GERMAN MILITARY SYMBOLS

January 1944
Intelligence Service
— War Department —

The Naval & Military Press Ltd

Published by

The Naval & Military Press Ltd
Unit 5 Riverside, Brambleside
Bellbrook Industrial Estate
Uckfield, East Sussex
TN22 1QQ England

Tel: +44 (0)1825 749494

www.naval-military-press.com
www.nmarchive.com

In reprinting in facsimile from the original, any imperfections are inevitably reproduced and the quality may fall short of modern type and cartographic standards.

NOT TO BE PUBLISHED

NOTICE

The contents of this volume will not be communicated to the public or to the press, but may be given to any person known to be loyal to the United States.

Changes, corrections, or any suggestions for the improvement of this text should be sent directly to the Central European Branch, Military Intelligence Service, War Department, Washington, D. C.

TABLE OF CONTENTS

	Page
SECTION I—EXPLANATION OF GERMAN MILITARY SYMBOLS	1
SECTION II—MILITARY SYMBOLS	
I. Headquarters of Higher Echelons	9
II. Infantry:	
A. Headquarters	12
B. Units	13
C. Weapons	16
D. Groups:	
1. Example of a Diagrammatic Table of Organization	18
2. Examples of Map Symbols	18
III. Artillery:	
A. Headquarters	19
B. Units	20
C. Weapons:	
1. Guns and Cannons	23
2. Howitzers	25
3. Weapons of Foreign Origin	27
D. Examples of Map Symbols	27
E. Miscellaneous	27
IV. Cavalry and Reconnaissance:	
A. Headquarters	28
B. Units	29
C. Vehicles	31
D. Examples of Map Symbols	31
V. Mountain:	
A. Headquarters	33
B. Units	33
C. Groups:	
1. Example of a Diagrammatic Table of Organization	35
2. Examples of Map Symbols	35

CONTENTS

	Page
VI. Panzer:	
A. Headquarters	36
B. Units	37
C. Tanks	40
D. Groups:	
1. Example of a Diagrammatic Table of Organization	41
2. Example of Map Symbols	41
E. Vehicles	42
VII. Engineer:	
A. Headquarters	43
B. Units	43
C. Groups:	
1. Example of a Diagramatic Table of Organization	46
2. Examples of Map Symbols	47
VIII. Railway Engineer:	
A. Headquarters	48
B. Units	48
IX. Fortress Engineer:	
A. Headquarters	51
B. Units	51
X. Technical:	
A. Headquarters	53
B. Units	53
C. Example of a Diagramatic Table of Organization	54
XI. Construction:	
A. Headquarters	55
B. Units	55
XII. Road Construction:	
A. Headquarters	56
B. Units	56
XIII. Signals:	
A. Headquarters	57
B. Units:	
1. Signal	59
2. Telephone and Telegraph	60
3. Radio	61
4. Interception	61
5. Miscellaneous	62
6. Propaganda	62
C. Installations	62

CONTENTS V

XIII. Signals—Continued.
    D. Sub-units:
        1. Telephone, Telegraph, and Teletype: Page
            a. Detachments 63
            b. Stations 65
            c. Lines 65
        2. Radio:
            a. Detachments 66
            b. Stations 67
            c. Methods of Operation 67
        3. Interception:
            a. Detachments 67
            b. Stations 68
        4. Other Methods of Communication 68
        5. Miscellaneous 69
XIV. Chemical:
    A. Headquarters 70
    B. Units 70
    C. Groups:
        1. Example of a Diagramatic Table of Organization 71
        2. Examples of Map Symbols 72
XV. Transport:
    A. Headquarters 73
    B. Units 73
    C. Groups:
        1. Example of a Diagramatic Table of Organization 74
        2. Examples of Map Symbols 75
    D. Trains of Combat Troops 75
XVI. Survey and Map Printing:
    A. Headquarters 76
    B. Units 76
    C. Installations 77
XVII. Services:
    A. Supply:
        1. Headquarters 78
        2. Units 80
        3. Installations 82
    B. Administrative:
        1. Units 85
        2. Installations 86

CONTENTS

XVII. Services—Continued.
    C. Medical: **Page**

	Page
C. Medical:	
1. Headquarters	87
2. Units	88
3. Miscellaneous	90
D. Veterinary	90
E. Postal:	
1. Headquarters	92
2. Units	92
F. Provost:	
1. Headquarters	93
2. Units	93
XVIII. Miscellaneous:	
A. Tactical Boundaries	94
B. Railroads and Transport	94
C. Obstacles:	
1. Mines	97
2. Miscellaneous	98
D. River Crossing:	
1. Crossing Points	101
2. Bridges	102
E. Defensive Positions	102
F. Miscellaneous	105
XIX. Air:	
A. Higher Headquarters	106
B. Flying Corps:	
1. Headquarters	107
2. Units	108
C. Signals:	
1. Headquarters	110
2. Units	110
3. Permanent Signals Ground Organization	111
4. Miscellaneous	111
D. Antiaircraft Artillery:	
1. Headquarters	112
2. Units	113
3. Weapons	115
E. Parachute Units	116
F. Air Bases	116
APPENDIX I—Ground Panel Signals Used By Troops For Air Communication	117
APPENDIX II—Nonofficial Auxiliary Signs	120
SECTION III—DOCUMENTS	125
ADDENDA	143

SECTION I

Explanation of German Military Symbols

1. The German Armed Forces use military symbols to a wide extent on their maps and charts, on task force tables of organization, on direction and location sign posts in combat zones, and even on armament and equipment. A thorough knowledge of these symbols, as well as the principles on which they are formulated, will assist intelligence personnel in making German identifications in combat.

2. German military symbols are designed to resemble the armament and establishments which they represent. The more complicated symbols are simply a logical development of the simple basic ones. Once the system of German military symbols is understood, intelligence personnel can deduce the meaning of unknown and new symbols.

3. The system of German military symbols will be explained by illustrative examples in the following paragraphs.

4. Particular attention is called to the symbols with a thickened line. They represent a unit of company strength.

5. Here is the basic German military symbol for a heavy machine gun: ⊥ By thickening the center line, the symbol represents a Machine Gun Company: ⊥

6. Herewith is the basic symbol for a gun: ı|ı It will

now be explained how this symbol is developed to represent the various types of guns and the organizations which man them.

a. The basic symbol for an infantry howitzer (75-mm Howitzer in the 13th Company of an Infantry Regiment) is as follows: ⫯ By thickening the center line, the symbol represents the Infantry Howitzer Company: ⫯

b. The basic gun symbol ⫯ , with a forked base represents an antitank gun: ⫯ Likewise, the addition of a circle represents an antiaircraft gun: ⫯

c. The addition of an extra line to a gun symbol usually indicates a larger caliber. Thus, a 75-mm infantry howitzer: ⫯ becomes a 150-mm infantry howitzer by the addition of another line to the symbol: ⫯ Also, the symbol for a 50-mm infantry mortar: ⌒ becomes the symbol for the 81-mm mortar: ⌒

7. A motorized unit is indicated by two small wheels on the unit symbol: ⫯ ⊶ ⫯ A partially motorized unit is represented by one wheel only: ⫯ = Partially

Motorized Telephone Company. Self-propelled mounts are represented by the symbol: ⊂⊃ . Thus, ▶ = Anti-tank Battalion Headquarters on Self-propelled Mount.

8. Command Posts or unit headquarters are shown by flag symbols. The shape and marking of the flag denotes the size of the command. Thus:

⚑ General Headquarters.

⚑ Army Group Headquarters.

⚑ Army Headquarters.

⚑ Corps Headquarters.

⚑ Divisional Headquarters.

⚑ Brigade Headquarters.

⚑ Regimental Headquarters.

⚑ Battalion Headquarters.

⚑ Company Commander.

9. Arms and Services have their own distinguishing symbols:

⋈------ Air.

o.--- Antiaircraft Artillery.

GERMAN MILITARY SYMBOLS

▷ ------ Antitank.

⚲ ▱ --- Armored.

⑆ -------- Artillery.

▭ ------ Battalion Strength.

⌐ ◪ ---- Cavalry and Reconnaissance.

⊏⊐ ------ Company Strength.

⚒ ------ Construction.

⊗ -------- Cyclist.

▭ ------ Depot or Park.

⇡ -------- Engineer.

⇡F -------- Fortress Engineer.

⊶▭ ----- Half-tracked.

✚ -------- Medical.

⌧ ------ Military Police.

⊗ ------ Motorcycle.

⊤°⊶⊕⊕ Motorized.

⚲ --------- Motor Transport.

▲ -------- Mountain.

⬗ ------ Parachute.

EXPLANATION OF GERMAN MILITARY SYMBOLS

--o-- ⚯ ..... Partly Motorized.

↗ .... Radio.

● .... Railway.

⇞ .... Railway Engineer.

↑ ▯ ..... Signal.

△ .... Smoke or Chemical Warfare Service.

⊤ .... Supply.

⋈ ▽ ... Survey.

Υ .... Telephone.

⊂⊃ ..... Tracked (Self-propelled Mount).

⚲ .... Traffic Control.

⊠ .... Train.

⊏⊐ ..... Transport Column.

⚘ .... Veterinary.

10. Basic Symbols for Weapons:

·|· ...... Machine Gun.

𝚪 .... Mortar.

⫼ .... Infantry Howitzer.

⚲ .... Flame-Thrower.

⊥ .... Antitank Rifle.

GERMAN MILITARY SYMBOLS

⚵ ──────── Antitank Gun.

⫯ ──────── Field Gun.

⚶ ──────── Field Howitzer.

│ ──────── Medium Gun (100 mm).

As previously indicated, these basic symbols can be supplemented by adding ∩ ─ ∧ ○. Each addition of one of these signs indicates an increase in caliber:

⚔ Heavy Machine Gun.
⌠ Heavy Mortar.

11. Basic symbols for weapons, symbols for arms and services, and the flags of headquarters may all be combined. Here, for example, is an illustration of the flexibility and adaptability of the German system of military symbols: 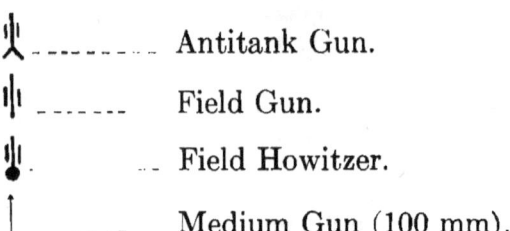 This character represents a Mountain Artillery Battalion Headquarters. Note the combination of three elements, e. g., ▶ (Battalion Headquarters), ⫯ (Artillery), and ▲ (Mountain).

12. Supplementary letters which are used to show special employment (F, Gr, Ls, Sich, St, Str, Wa, etc.) are always found on the left of the symbol, e. g. ₣▶ Fortress Engineer Regimental Headquarters.

Other letters, used to denote the nature and organic assignment of a formation, are found on the right of the symbol: ⚑PA Motorized Army Signal Battalion Headquarters.

In a few exceptional cases, the letters are found above, below, or within the military symbol.

13. Supplementary numbers.

a. Headquarters of Armies, Divisions, Regiments, Independent Battalions, Companies, etc. carry an arabic numeral on the right side of the military symbol as a designation of the unit, e. g., ⚑10 10th Infantry Regiment.

b. Headquarters of Army Corps and Battalions within a Regiment are shown by the use of Roman numerals:

⚑VIII VIII Army Corps Headquarters.

⚑II/67 2nd Battalion, 67th Infantry Regiment.

c. A figure below a military symbol sign indicates the number of weapons in a unit or the tonnage capacity of columns, ferries, and bridges:

†/3 3 Light Machine Guns.

⫼/2 2 Infantry Howitzers (75 mm).

14. It will be noticed that, in certain instances, there are alternate military symbols for the same subject. This is in no wise a deviation from a consistent pattern, but rather further testimony to the logic of the German system. Some German commander, not knowing the precise symbol, has put one together from well-known basic signs.

The resultant symbol is fully as comprehensible as the official one.

15. In the translation of German terms, an attempt has been made to approximate, as closely as possible, equivalent units in the Army of the United States. In many instances, however, no equivalents exist, necessitating a literal translation.

16. An effort has been made to employ only those German terms which are officially used to designate a particular military symbol. The absence of German opposite many of the symbols is explained by lack of authoritative nomenclature.

17. The following changes in nomenclature, arriving too late for inclusion in this book, should be noted:
> Infanterieregiment should read Grenadierregiment
> leichte Division should read Jägerdivision (except "leichte Afrika-division").

SECTION II
Military Symbols

I. HEADQUARTERS OF HIGHER ECHELONS

Military Symbol	German	U. S. Equivalent
	Oberkommando des Heeres	General Headquarters
	Heeresgruppenkommando	Army Group Headquarters
	Armeeoberkommando	Army Headquarters
	Korpskommando	Corps Headquarters
	Korpskommando (mot.)	Motorized Corps Headquarters
	Gebirgskorpskommando	Mountain Corps Headquarters
or	Panzerkorpskommando	Panzer Corps Headquarters
H.K.	Höheres Kommando	Headquarters of Force Equivalent to a Corps
r.H.	Befehlshaber des Rückwärtigen Heeresgebiets	Headquarters of Army Group Rear Area (Communications Zone)
	Kommando einer Infanteriedivision	Infantry Divisional Headquarters
	Kommando einer Infanteriedivision (mot.)	Motorized Infantry Divisional Headquarters

GERMAN MILITARY SYMBOLS

Military Symbol	German	U. S. Equivalent
	Kommando einer leichten Infanteriedivision	Light Infantry Divisional Headquarters
Sich	Kommando einer Sicherungsdivision	Line of Communications Divisional Headquarters
Ls	Kommando einer Landesschützendivision	Local Defense Divisional Headquarters
	Kommando einer Gebirgsdivision	Mountain Divisional Headquarters
	Kommando einer Panzerdivision	Panzer Divisional Headquarters
	Stab eines Artilleriekommandeurs	Corps or Army Artillery Command Staff
F		Inspector of Fortifications
r.A.	Kommandant des Rückwärtigen Armeegebietes	Headquarters of Army Rear Area (Communications Zone)
	Stab einer Infanteriebrigade	Infantry Brigade Headquarters
	Stab eines Artillerieführers	Divisional Artillery Commander's Headquarters
	Stab einer Kavalleriebrigade	Cavalry Brigade Headquarters
	Stab einer Panzerbrigade	Panzer Brigade Headquarters
	Stab einer Panzergrenadierbrigade	Motorized Rifle Brigade Headquarters in Panzer Division

Military Symbol	German	U. S. Equivalent
	Stab eines Küstenartilleriekommandeurs	Coast Defense Artillery Headquarters (Status of Brigade)
	Stab eines Festungsartilleriekommandeurs	Fortress Artillery Headquarters
	Stab eines Eisenbahnpionierkommandeurs	Railway Engineer Headquarters
	Stab eines Festungspionierkommandeurs	Fortress Engineer Headquarters
	Oberbaustab	Construction Staff (Status of Brigade)
		Higher Echelons Signal Headquarters

II. INFANTRY
A. Headquarters:

Military Symbol	German	U. S. Equivalent
▛	Stab eines Infanterieregiments	Infantry Regimental Headquarters
Sich ▛	Stab eines Sicherungsregiments.	Line of Communications Regimental Headquarters
Gr ▛	Stab eines Grenzwachtregiments	Frontier (Guard) Regimental Headquarters
Ls ▛	Stab eines Landesschützenregiments	Local Defense Regimental Headquarters
▛₀₀	Stab eines Infanterieregiments (mot.)	Motorized Infantry Regimental Headquarters
▶	Stab eines Infanteriebataillons	Infantry Battalion Headquarters
▶₀₀	Stab eines Infanteriebataillons (mot.)	Motorized Infantry Battalion Headquarters
▶ ○	Stab eines Radfahrerbataillons (tmot.)	Bicycle Battalion Headquarters (Partly Motorized)
Sich ▶	Stab eines Sicherungsbataillons	Line of Communications Battalion Headquarters
Gr ▶	Stab eines Grenzwachtbataillons	Frontier (Guard) Battalion Headquarters
Ls ▶	Stab eines Landesschützenbataillons	Local Defense Battalion Headquarters
Wa ▶	Stab eines Wachbataillons	Guard Battalion Headquarters

MILITARY SYMBOLS 13

Military Symbol	German	U. S. Equivalent
Feld |Ers	Stab eines Feldersatzbataillons	Replacement Battalion Headquarters (In Field)
	Stab eines Maschinengewehrbataillons (mot.)	Motorized Machine Gun Battalion Headquarters
	Stab eines Kradschützenbataillons	Motorcycle Rifle Battalion Headquarters
	Kompanieführer	Company Commander
	Kompanieführer (mot.)	Company Commander (Motorized Unit)
	Kradschützenkompanieführer	Motorcycle Company Commander
	Radfahrerschwadronführer	Bicycle Company Commander

B. Units:

	Schützenkompanie	Rifle Company
	Schützenkompanie (mot.)	Motorized Rifle Company
Sich	Sicherungskompanie	Line of Communications Company
Gr	Grenzwachtkompanie	Frontier (Guard) Company
Ls	Landesschützenkompanie	Local Defense Company
Wa	Wachkompanie	Guard Company
St	Stabskompanie	Headquarters Company
St	Stabskompanie (mot.)	Motorized Headquarters Company

14   GERMAN MILITARY SYMBOLS

Military Symbol	German	U. S. Equivalent
[S]	Schwere Kompanie (mot.)	Motorized Heavy Weapons Company
	Panzerabwehrkompanie (mot.)	Motorized Antitank Company
	Maschinengewehrkompanie	Machine Gun Company
	Maschinengewehrkompanie (mot.)	Motorized Machine Gun Company
Gr	Grenzwacht-Maschinengewehrkompanie	Frontier (Guard) Machine Gun Company
	M. G. Kp., vierspännig	Machine Gun Company With Vehicles Drawn by Four Horses
or	Kraftrad-(Krad-) Maschinengewehrkompanie	Motorcycle Machine Gun Company
	Kradschützenkompanie	Motorcycle Rifle Company
l	Leichte Kradschützenkompanie	Light Motorcycle Rifle Company
(s)	Schwere Kradschützenkompanie	Motorcycle Heavy Weapons Company
	Radfahrerkompanie	Bicycle Company
l	Sicherungs-Radfahrerkompanie	Line of Communications Bicycle Company
a	Wachradfahrerkompanie	Guard Bicycle Company
	Infanteriegeschützkompanie	Infantry Howitzer Company

MILITARY SYMBOLS

Military Symbol	German	U. S. Equivalent
	Infanteriegeschütz-kompanie (mot.)	Motorized Infantry Howitzer Company
	Schwere Infanteriegeschützkompanie	Heavy Infantry Howitzer Company on Self-propelled Mounts
	Kradschützenzug	Motorcycle Rifle Platoon
	Kradmeldetrupp	Motorcycle Detachment at Regimental Headquarters
	Infanterie-Reiterzug	Mounted Infantry Reconnaissance Platoon (Horse)
	Nachrichtenzug bei Stäben	Headquarters Signal Platoon
	Nachrichtenzug bei Stäben (mot.)	Motorized Headquarters Signal Platoon
	Kraftradmeldezug (Kradmeldezug)	Motorcycle Messenger Platoon
	Schützenzug	Rifle Platoon
or	Granatwerferzug	Heavy Mortar Platoon
	Granatwerferzug (mot.)	Motorized Heavy Mortar Platoon
	Infanteriepionierzug	Infantry Combat Engineer Platoon
	Infanteriepionierzug (mot.)	Motorized Infantry Combat Engineer Platoon
	Panzerabwehrzug	Antitank Platoon

GERMAN MILITARY SYMBOLS

Military Symbol	German	U. S. Equivalent
	Panzerabwehrzug (mot.)	Motorized Antitank Platoon
	Leichter Infanteriegeschützzug (mot.)	Motorized Light Infantry Howitzer Platoon
	Schwerer Infanteriegeschützzug (mot.)	Motorized Heavy Infantry Howitzer Platoon
	Schwerer Infanteriegeschützzug auf Selbstfahrlafetten	Heavy Infantry Howitzer Platoon on Self-propelled Mounts
	Leichte Infanteriekolonne	Infantry Light Transport Column
	Leichte Infanteriekolonne (mot.)	Infantry Light Transport Column (Motorized)

C. Weapons:

	Maschinengewehr or Leichtes M. G.	Machine Gun or Light Machine Gun
	Leichtes M. G. in Stellung	Light Machine Gun in Position
	Schweres M. G.	Heavy Machine Gun
	Schweres M. G. in Stellung	Heavy Machine Gun in Position
	Leichter Granatwerfer	Light Mortar (50 mm)
	Schwerer Granatwerfer	Heavy Mortar (81 mm)
	Leichtes Infanteriegeschütz	Light Infantry Howitzer (75 mm)

MILITARY SYMBOLS

Military Symbol	German	U. S. Equivalent
	Schweres Infanteriegeschütz	Heavy Infantry Howitzer (150 mm)
	Panzerbüchse	Antitank Rifle
	Panzerbüchse 41	Antitank Rifle 41
	2 cm Panzerabwehrgeschütz	20-mm Antitank Gun
or	Panzerabwehrkanone (3.7 cm)	37-mm Antitank Gun
	Panzerabwehrkanone (in Stellung)	37-mm Antitank Gun in Position
	4.7 cm Panzerabwehrgeschütz	47-mm Antitank Gun
	4.7 cm Panzerabwehrgeschütz	47-mm Antitank Gun (Czech)
or	5 cm Pak/Flak	50-mm Antitank/Antiaircraft Gun
	7.5 cm Pak/Flak	75-mm Antitank/Antiaircraft Gun
R	7.62 cm Pak/Flak	76.2-mm Antitank/Antiaircraft Gun
	8.8 cm Pak/Flak	88-mm Antitank/Antiaircraft Gun

D. Groups:

1. Example of a Diagrammatic Table of Organization:

Military Symbol	German	U. S. Equivalent
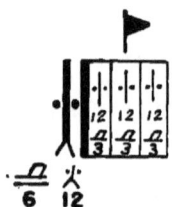	Infanteriebataillon	Infantry Battalion (showing composition of 3 Rifle Companies, each with 12 Light Machine Guns and 3 Light Mortars, 1 Heavy Weapons Company, with 12 Heavy Machine Guns and 6 Heavy Mortars)

2. Examples of Map Symbols:

	German	U. S. Equivalent
	Infanteriebataillon	Infantry Battalion (1st Battalion, 21st Regiment)
	Maschinengewehrbataillon (mot.)	10th Motorized Machine Gun Battalion
	Infanterie-Marschkolonne	Infantry March Column
	Marschkolonne Motorisierter Infanterie	Motorized Infantry March Column
	Einzelner Schütze	Individual Rifleman
	Feldposten, Spähtrupp	Patrol
	Feldwache	Picket
	Beobachtungstelle	Observation Post
	Schützennest	Group of Entrenched Riflemen
	Schützen in Entwicklung	Deployed Riflemen

III. ARTILLERY
A. Headquarters:

Military Symbol	German	U. S. Equivalent
	Stab eines Artillerieregiments	Field Artillery Regimental Headquarters
	Stab eines Artillerieregiments (mot.)	Motorized Field Artillery Regimental Headquarters
	Stab eines reitenden Artillerieregiments	Horse Artillery Regimental Headquarters
	Stab eines Gebirgsartillerieregiments	Mountain Artillery Regimental Headquarters
		Motorized Artillery Regimental Headquarters in Panzer Division
	Stab eines Küstenartillerieregiments	Coast Artillery Regimental Headquarters
	Stab eines Leichtgeschützregiments	Light Artillery Regimental Headquarters
	Stab einer Artillerieabteilung	Field Artillery Battalion Headquarters
	Stab einer Artillerieabteilung (mot.)	Motorized Field Artillery Battalion Headquarters
	Stab einer reitenden Artillerieabteilung	Horse Artillery Battalion Headquarters
Bb	Stab einer Beobachtungsabteilung (mot.)	Motorized Artillery Observation Battalion Headquarters

19

GERMAN MILITARY SYMBOLS

Military Symbol	German	U. S. Equivalent
	Stab einer Gebirgsartillerieabteilung	Mountain Artillery Battalion Headquarters
		Motorized Field Artillery Battalion Headquarters in Panzer Division
	Stab einer Sturmgeschützabteilung	Assault Gun Battalion Headquarters
	Stab einer Küstenartillerieabteilung	Coast Artillery Battalion Headquarters
	Stab einer Leichtgeschützabteilung	Light Gun Battalion Headquarters
	Batterieführer	Battery Commander

B. Units:

	Stabsbatterie	Headquarters Battery
	Stabsbatterie (mot.)	Motorized Headquarters Battery
	Gebirgsstabsbatterie	Mountain Headquarters Battery
	Reitende Stabsbatterie	Headquarters Battery in Horse Artillery Unit
		Motorized Headquarters Battery in a Motorized or Panzer Unit
	Stabsbatterie einer Beobachtungsabteilung (mot.)	Motorized Headquarters Battery of a Motorized Artillery Observation Battalion

MILITARY SYMBOLS

Military Symbol	German	U. S. Equivalent
[St]	Stabsbatterie einer Sturmgeschützabteilung	Headquarters Battery of an Assault Gun Battalion
[Li]	Lichtmessbatterie (mot.)	Motorized Flash Ranging Battery
[Bb]	Beobachtungsbatterie (mot.)	Motorized Artillery Observation Battery (in Panzer Division)
[Sch]	Schallmessbatterie (mot.)	Motorized Artillery Sound Ranging Battery
	Vermessungsbatterie (mot.)	Motorized Artillery Survey Battery
	Ballonbatterie (mot.)	Motorized Balloon Battery
	Batterie L. F. H. (7.5 cm)	Light Field Howitzer Battery (75 mm)
	L. F. H. (16) Batterie in Stellung (10.5 cm)	Light Field Howitzer (16) Battery in Position (105 mm)
	Batterie L. F. H. (18) in Stellung (10.5 cm)	Light Field Howitzer (18) Battery in Position (105 mm)
	Batterie langer schweren Feldhaubitzen	Long Medium Field Howitzer (13) Battery
	Batterie schwerer Haubitzen	Medium Howitzer (18) Battery
	.Batterie Feldkanonen	Field Gun Battery

GERMAN MILITARY SYMBOLS

Military Symbol	German	U. S. Equivalent
	Gebirgsbatterie	Mountain Battery
	Reitende Batterie Feldkanonen	Horse Battery of Field Guns
	Reitende Batterie Feldkanonen in Stellung	Horse Battery of Field Guns in Position
	Batterie 10 cm Kanonen	100-mm Gun Battery
	Batterie 21 cm Mörser	210-mm Mortar Battery
	Nachrichtenzug des Stabes eines Regiments oder einer Abteilung	Regimental or Battalion Headquarters Signal Platoon
or	Wetterzug (mot.)	Motorized Meteorological Platoon
		Motorized Meteorological Platoon (Air Currents and Air Pressures)
		Motorized Medium Calibration Platoon
	Vermessungszug (mot.)	Motorized Artillery Survey Platoon
	Artillerievermsseungstrupp	Artillery Survey Detachment
or	Artillerievermessungstrupp (mot.)	Motorized Artillery Survey Detachment

Military Symbol	German	U. S. Equivalent
	Gebirgsartillerievermessungstrupp	Mountain Artillery Survey Detachment
or	Druckereitrupp (mot.)	Motorized Printing Detachment
	Wettertrupp (mot.)	Motorized Meteorological Detachment
		Motorized Light Calibration Detachment
or	Leichte Artilleriekolonne	Light Transport Column of Artillery
or	Leichte Artilleriekolonne (mot.)	Motorized Light Transport Column of Artillery
	Leichte Gebirgsartilleriekolonne (mot.)	Motorized Light Transport Column of Mountain Artillery
	Kraftzug-Artilleriekolonne	Tractor Drawn Artillery Supply Column (Diesel)
		Pack Supply Column of a Light Artillery Battery in a Motorized Division
		Pack Supply Column of a Motorized Medium Artillery Battery in a Motorized Division

C. Weapons:

1. Guns and Cannons:

	Feldkanone (7.5 cm)	Field Gun (75 mm)

24 GERMAN MILITARY SYMBOLS

Military Symbol	German	U. S. Equivalent
	F. K. 16 (7.5 cm)	Field Cannon 16 (75 mm)
	F. K. 18 (7.5 cm)	Field Gun 18 (75 mm)
	Leichtgeschütz	Light Gun (75 mm)
		Mountain Gun 15 (75 mm)
		Mountain Gun 36 (75 mm)
	Sturmgeschütz (7.5 cm)	Assault Gun (75 mm)
	10 cm K.	100-mm Cannon
	10 cm K. 17	100-mm Cannon 17 (or new Model 17/04)
	10.5 cm K. 18	105-mm Cannon 18
		Coast Defense 120-mm Cannon
	15 cm K. 16 (mot.)	Motorized 150-mm Cannon 16
	15 cm K. 18 (mot.)	150-mm Cannon 18 (Motorized)
	15 cm K. 39 (mot.)	150-mm Cannon 39 (Motorized)
		150-mm Cannon on Howitzer Mounting (Motorized)
	15 cm Eisenbahngeschütz	150-mm Railway Gun

Military Symbol	German	U. S. Equivalent
		170-mm Gun on Howitzer Mounting (Motorized)
	17 cm Eisenbahngeschütz	170-mm Railway Gun
	20.3 cm Eisenbahngeschütz	203-mm Railway Gun
		210-mm Gun 38 (Motorized.
		210-mm Gun 39 (Motorized)
	Eisenbahngeschütz 12	Railway Gun 12
		240-mm Gun (Motorized)
		240-mm Railway Gun (Theodor or Theodor-Bruno)
		280-mm Railway Gun (Short, Long, or Heavy Bruno Type)
	Eisenbahngeschütz 5	Railway Gun 5
		305-mm Fixed Gun

2. Howitzers:

	L. F. H. (10.5 cm)	Light Field Howitzer (105 mm)
	L. F. H. auf Selbstfahrlafette	Light Field Howitzer on Self-propelled Mount

Military Symbol	German	U. S. Equivalent
	L. F. H. 16 (10.5 cm)	Light Field Howitzer 16 (105 mm)
	L. F. H. 18 (10.5 cm)	Light Field Howitzer 18 (105 mm)
	L. F. H. 18 (mot.)	Light Field Howitzer 18 (Motorized)
		120-mm Howitzer
		Medium Howitzer (150 mm)
	Lg. s. F. H. 13 (15 cm)	Long Medium Field Howitzer 13
	S. F. H. 18 (mot.) (15 cm)	Medium Field Howitzer 18 (150 mm) (Motorized)
		210-mm Howitzer (Motorized)
		Long 210-mm Howitzer (Motorized)
		210-mm How 18 (Motorized)
		240-mm Howitzer 39 (Motorized)
		305-mm Howitzer (Motorized)
		Howitzer M. 1 (Motorized)
		420-mm Howitzer (Motorized)

MILITARY SYMBOLS 27

Military Symbol	German	U. S. Equivalent
⊖		"Gamma" Howitzer (Motorized)

3. **Weapons of Foreign Origin:**

In the case of guns of foreign origin, the military symbol for the appropriate caliber is used together with the letter showing the country of origin.

↑t	10 cm K.	100-mm Cannon (Czech)
↑p		Medium Howitzer (Polish)
↑f 	15 cm K.	150-mm Cannon (French)

D. **Examples of Map Symbols:**

▭▭▭▭ or ⇐	Artillerie-Marschkolonne	Artillery March Column
╷ I/I		1st Battalion, 1st Regiment (Light Field Howitzers)
▲A	Armee-Beobachtungsstelle	Army Observation Post

E. **Miscellaneous:**

⊕	Lichtmessstelle	Flash Ranging Station
⊖ or Ⓢ	Schallmessstelle	Artillery Sound Ranging Station
Ⓥ		Warning Post
ⓟ		Wagon Lines

IV. CAVALRY AND RECONNAISSANCE

A. Headquarters:

Military Symbol	German	U. S. Equivalent
	Stab eines Kavallerie- (Reiter-) Regiments	Horse Cavalry Regimental Headquarters
	Stab einer Aufklärungsabteilung einer Infanteriedivision	Headquarters of Reconnaissance Battalion of Infantry Division
	Stab einer Aufklärungsabteilung einer Infanteriedivision (tmot.)	Headquarters of Partly Motorized Reconnaissance Battalion of Infantry Division
	Stab einer Aufklärungsabteilung einer Infanteriedivision (mot.)	Headquarters of Motorized Reconnaissance Battalion of Infantry Division
	Stab eines Radfahrerbataillons (tmot.)	Bicycle Battalion Headquarters (Partly Motorized)
	Stab einer Gebirgsaufklärungsabteilung	Headquarters of Partly Motorized Reconnaissance Battalion of Mountain Division
	Panzerspäh - Aufklärungsabteilung	Headquarters of Armored-Car Reconnaissance Battalion
	Führer einer Schwadron	Troop Commander
	Führer einer Schwadron (mot.)	Troop Commander (Motorized)

Military Symbol	German	U. S. Equivalent
	Führer einer M. G.-Schwadron	Machine Gun Troop Commander
	Führer einer Radfahrerschwadron	Bicycle Troop Commander
	Führer einer Panzerspähschwadron	Armored-Car Commander

B. Units:

	Reiterschwadron	Horse Cavalry Troop
or	Maschinengewehrschwadron.	Cavalry Machine Gun Troop
	Maschinengewehrschwadron (mot.)	Motorized Cavalry Machine Gun Troop
	Kavallerie-Geschützschwadron.	Cavalry Howitzer Troop
A	Reiteraufklärungsschwadron	Horse Cavalry Reconnaissance Troop
	Radfahrerschwadron	Bicycle Troop
A	Radfahrer-Aufklärungsschwadron.	Bicycle Reconnaissance Troop
	Gebirgsradfahrer-Aufklärungsschwadron	Mountain Bicycle Reconnaissance Troop
	Panzerspähschwadron	Armored-Car Troop
	Panzerspähschwadron einer Panzeraufklärungsabteilung	Armored-Car Troop in Armored Reconnaissance Battalion

Military Symbol	German	U. S. Equivalent
	Kradschützenschwadron	Motorcycle Troop
	Kradschützenschwadron eines Panzerverbandes	Motorcycle Troop in an Armored Formation
	Schwerwaffenschwadron (mot.)	Motorized Heavy Weapons Troop
	Schwerwaffen - Radfahrerschwadron (mot.)	Motorized Heavy Weapons Troop of a Bicycle Squadron
	Gebirgs - Schwerwaffenschwadron (mot.)	Motorized Mountain Heavy Weapons Troop
	Schwerwaffenschwadron eines Panzerverbandes	Motorized Heavy Weapons Troop in an Armored Formation
	Kavallerie-Panzerabwehrzug	Cavalry Antitank Platoon
	Kavallerie-Panzerabwehrzug (mot.)	Motorized Cavalry Antitank Platoon
or	Kavallerie-Geschützzug	Cavalry Howitzer Platoon
or	Kavallerie-Pionierzug (mot.)	Motorized Cavalry Combat Engineer Platoon
	Kavallerie - Nachrichtenzug (tmot.)	Partly Motorized Cavalry Signal Platoon
or or	Kavallerie-Nachrichtenzug (mot.)	Motorized Cavalry Signal Platoon
	Nachrichtenzug einer Aufklärungsabteilung (mot.)	Motorized Signal Platoon of a Reconnaissance Battalion

MILITARY SYMBOLS 31

Military Symbol	German	U. S. Equivalent
	Panzerspähzug	Armored-Car Platoon
	Kradschützenzug	Motorcycle Rifle Platoon
	Granatwerferzug (mot.)	Motorized Heavy Mortar Platoon
	Leichte Kavalleriekolonne	Light Cavalry Transport Column
	Leichte Panzerspähkolonne	Light Transport Column in an Armored-Car Unit

C. Vehicles:

	Leichter Panzerspähwagen	Light Armored-Car
	Leichter Panzerspähwagen (Französisch)	Light Armored-Car (French)
	Schwerer Panzerspähwagen	Heavy Armored-Car
		Heavy Armored-Car (With Radio)

D. Examples of Map Symbols:

	Reiterposten	Mounted Trooper
	Reiterspähtrupp, Reiterfeldposten	Cavalry Patrol
F.W.	Reiterfeldwache	Cavalry Picket
	Radfahrerfeldposten, Radfahrerspähtrupp	Bicycle Patrol
	Bewegung von Kavallerie	Movement of Cavalry

GERMAN MILITARY SYMBOLS

Military Symbol	German	U. S. Equivalent
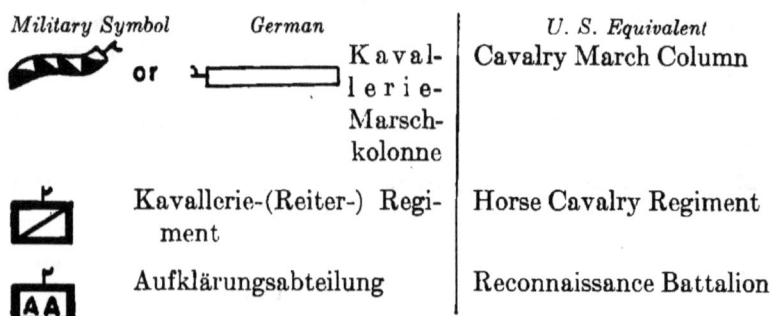	Kavallerie-Marschkolonne	Cavalry March Column
	Kavallerie-(Reiter-) Regiment	Horse Cavalry Regiment
	Aufklärungsabteilung	Reconnaissance Battalion

V. MOUNTAIN

A. Headquarters:

Military Symbol	German	U. S. Equivalent
	Stab eines Gebirgsjägerregiments	Mountain Infantry Regimental Headquarters
	Stab eines Gebirgsjägerbataillons	Mountain Infantry Battalion Headquarters
	Stab eines Gebirgs-Radfahrer-Bataillons(tmot.)	Mountain Bicycle Battalion Headquarters (Partly Motorized)
	Stab einer Gebirgsflakartillerieabteilung (tmot.)	Mountain Antiaircraft Artillery Battalion Headquarters (Partly Motorized)
	Führer einer Gebirgsjägerkompanie	Mountain Rifle Company Commander
	Führer einer Gebirgsradfahrerkompanie	Mountain Bicycle Company Commander

B. Units:

	Gebirgsjägerkompanie	Mountain Rifle Company
	Gebirgsjägermaschinengewehrkompanie	Machine Gun Company of Mountain Infantry Battalion
	Gebirgsstabskompanie	Mountain Headquarters Company
	Gebirgsradfahrerkompanie	Mountain Bicycle Company

Military Symbol	German	U. S. Equivalent
	Schwere Gebirgsradfahrerkompanie (mot.)	Heavy Weapons Company of a Mountain Bicycle Battalion
	Gebirgsflakbatterie (2 cm) (mot.)	Motorized Mountain Antiaircraft Artillery Battery (20 mm)
	Gebirgspanzerabwehrkompanie (mot.)	Motorized Mountain Antitank Company
	Gebirgsgranatwerferzug	Mountain Heavy Mortar Platoon
	Gebirgsgeschützzug	Mountain Howitzer Platoon
or	Nachrichtenzug bei Stäben von Gebirgseinheiten	Signal Platoon with Mountain Units Headquarters
	Gebirgsradfahrerzug	Mountain Bicycle Platoon
	Leichte Gebirgskolonne	Light Mountain Transport Column
	Leichte Gebirgsjägerkolonne	Mountain Infantry Light Transport Column

MILITARY SYMBOLS 35

C. Groups:

1. Example of a Diagrammatic Table of Organization:

Military Symbol   *German*   *U. S. Equivalent*

    Gebirgsjägerbataillon
    Mountain Infantry Battalion Consisting of:
        Battalion Headquarters
        3 Mountain Rifle Companies, each with:
            12 Light Machine Guns
            3 Light Mortars
            2 Heavy Mortars
        1 Mountain Machine Gun Company with
            12 Heavy Machine Guns
        1 Headquarters Company with
            1 Engineer Platoon with 4 Light Machine Guns
            1 Signal Platoon
            1 Howitzer Platoon with 2 Light Howitzers
        2 Examples of Map Symbols

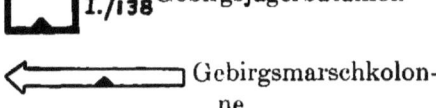

I./138	Gebirgsjägerbataillon	1st Battalion, 138th Mountain Rifle Regiment
	Gebirgsmarschkolonne	March Column of Mountain Troops

VI. PANZER
A. Headquarters:

Military Symbol	German	U. S. Equivalent
	Stab eines Panzerregiments	Tank Regimental Headquarters
	Stab eines Panzergrenadierregiments (mot.)	Infantry Regimental Headquarters (in Panzer Division).
		Armored Infantry Regimental Headquarters
		Artillery Regimental Headquarters (in Panzer Division)
	Stab einer Panzerabteilung	Tank Battalion Headquarters
	Stab einer Panzerflammenwerferabteilung	Armored Flamethrower Battalion Headquarters
	Stab einer Panzerabwehrabteilung auf Selbstfahrlafetten	Antitank Battalion Headquarters on Self-propelled Mounts
	Stab eines Panzergrenadierbataillons (mot.)	Infantry Battalion Headquarters (in Panzer Division)
		Armored Infantry Battalion Headquarters

Military Symbol	German	U. S. Equivalent
	Stab eines Kradschützenbataillons	Motorcycle Rifle Battalion Headquarters (in Panzer Division)
	Stab einer Aufklärungsabteilung (mot.)	Motorized Reconnaissance Battalion Headquarters (in Panzer Division)
	Führer einer Kompanie der Kraftfahrkampftruppe	Company Commander (in Armored Force)
		Armored Infantry Company Commander
	Führer einer Panzerkompanie	Tank Company Commander
	Führer einer Panzerflammenwerferkompanie	Armored Flamethrower Company Commander

B. Units:

	German	U. S. Equivalent
	Panzerabteilung	Tank Battalion (3 Companies)
	Panzerabteilung	Tank Battalion (2 Light Companies, 1 Medium Company)
	Panzerabteilung	Tank Battalion
	Panzerabwehrabteilung (mot.)	Motorized Antitank Battalion
	Aufklärungsabteilung (mot.)	Motorized Reconnaissance Battalion

GERMAN MILITARY SYMBOLS

Military Symbol	German	U. S. Equivalent
	Panzergrenadierbataillon (mot.)	Motorized Infantry Battalion (in Panzer Division)
	Panzerkompanie	Tank Company
	Leichte Panzerkompanie	Light Tank Company
	Mittlere Panzerkompanie	Medium Tank Company
	Panzerflammenwerferkompanie	Armored Flamethrower Company
	Panzerstabskompanie	Armored Headquarters Company
	Werkstattkompanie	Armored Maintenance Company
	Panzergrenadierkompanie (mot.)	Motorized Company (in Panzer Division)
		Armored Infantry Company
	Schwere Kompanie (mot.)	Motorized Heavy Weapons Company (in Panzer Division)
		Armored Heavy Weapons Company
	Maschinengewehrkompanie (mot.)	Motorized Machine Gun Company (in Panzer Division)
		Armored Machine Gun Company

Military Symbol	German	U. S. Equivalent
	Infanteriegeschützkompanie (mot.)	Motorized Infantry Howitzer Company (in Panzer Division)
	Stabskompanie (mot.)	Motorized Headquarters Company (in Panzer Division)
		Armored Headquarters Company
	Panzerabwehrkompanie (mot.)	Motorized Antitank Company (in Panzer Division)
	Panzerabwehrkompanie auf Selbstfahrlafetten	Antitank Company on Self-propelled Mounts (in Panzer Division)
	Kradschützenkompanie	Motorcycle Rifle Company (in Panzer Division)
	Schwere Kradschützenkompanie	Motorcycle Heavy Weapons Company (in Panzer Division)
	Kradmaschinengewehrkompanie	Motorcycle Machine Gun Company (in Panzer Division)
	Schwerer Infanteriegeschützzug (mot.)	Motorized Heavy Infantry Howitzer Platoon (in Panzer Division)
	Pionierzug (mot.)	Motorized Combat Engineer Platoon (in Panzer Division)

Military Symbol	German	U. S. Equivalent
		Armored Combat Engineer Platoon
or	Zug Panzerkampfwagen	Tank Platoon
	Leichter Panzerzug	Light Tank Platoon
	Werkstattzug	Armored Maintenance Platoon
		Armored Recovery Platoon
	Nachrichtenzug bei Stäben (mot.)	Motorized Signal Platoon (in Panzer Division)
		Armored Signal Platoon
	Panzernachrichtenzug	Armored Signal Platoon
	Panzer-Gefechtstross	Armored Combat Train
	Eisenbahn-Panzerzug	Armored Train (Railway)

C. Tanks:

	Panzerkampfwagen I	Tank, Mark I
	Panzerkampfwagen II	Tank, Mark II
	Panzerkampfwagen II (Französisch)	Tank, Mark II (French; for Platoon Commander)
	Panzerkampfwagen III	Tank, Mark III

MILITARY SYMBOLS 41

Military Symbol	German	U. S. Equivalent
🯅	Panzerbefehlswagen	Command Tank
⊠ Br	Brückenträger - Panzerkampfwagen	Bridge Laying Tank in Armored Engineer Battalion
⊠	Panzerkampfwagen IV	Tk, Mark IV (for Company Commander)

D. Groups:
1. Example of a Diagramatic Table of Organization:

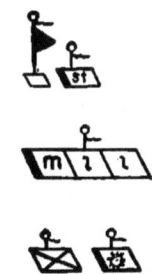

Tank Battalion, Consisting of:
  Headquarters
  Headquarters Company
  Tank Battalion
    2 Light Tank Companies
    1 Medium Tank Company
  Supply Train
  Maintenance Company

2. Examples of Map Symbols:

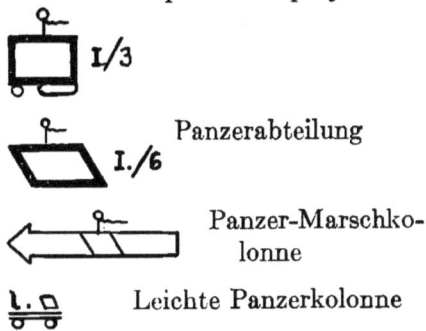

I/3		1st Battalion, 3rd Infantry Regiment (in Panzer Division)
I./6	Panzerabteilung	1st Battalion, 6th Tank Regiment
	Panzer-Marschkolonne	March Column of Tank Units
	Leichte Panzerkolonne	Light Transport Column of Armored Units

42 GERMAN MILITARY SYMBOLS

Military Symbol	German	U. S. Equivalent
E. Vehicles:		
	Panzerspähkompanie	Armored-Car Company
	Panzerspäheinheiten	Armored-Car Units
	Panzerspähwagen	Armored-Car
	Mittl. Panzer-Funktrupp	Medium Panzer Radio Detachment
	Kl. Panzer-Funktrupp	Small Panzer Radio Detachment
	L. Panzerspäh-Funktrupp	Light Armored-Car Radio Detachment
	Stabs-Raupenfahrzeug Nr. 251	Special Headquarters Vehicle #251
	Panzerspähwagen, 4 Rädrig-Nr. 260	4 Wheeled Armored-Car #260
	Panzerspähwagen, 4 Rädrig-Nr. 261	4 Wheeled Armored-Car #261
	Panzerspähwagen 8 Rädrig-Nr. 263	8 Wheeled Armored-Car #263

VII. ENGINEERS

A. Headquarters:

Military Symbol	German	U. S. Equivalent
	Stab eines Pionierregiments	Combat Engineer Regimental Headquarters
	Stab eines Pionierregiments (mot.)	Motorized Combat Engineer Regimental Headquarters
	Stab eines Pionierbataillons (tmot.)	Combat Engineer Battalion Headquarters (Partly Motorized)
	Stab eines Pionierbataillons (mot.)	Motorized Combat Engineer Battalion Headquarters
or Pz	Panzertruppe - Pionierbataillon	Armored Combat Engineer Battalion Headquarters
	Stab eines Gebirgspionierbataillons	Mountain Combat Engineer Battalion Headquarters
	Stab eines Pionierbrückenbataillons (tmot.)	Combat Engineer Bridging Battalion Headquarters (Partly Motorized)
	Kompanieführer einer Pionierkompanie	Combat Engineer Company Commander

B. Units:

	Pionierkompanie	Combat Engineer Company

43

Military Symbol	German	U. S. Equivalent
	Pionierkompanie (mot.)	Motorized Combat Engineer Company
	Gebirgspionierkompanie	Mountain Combat Engineer Company
	Brückenbaukompanie	Bridge Building Company
	Leichte Pionierkompanie (mot.)	Light Motorized Combat Engineer Company (In Armored Unit)
	Pionierpark	Combat Engineer Supply Depot Company
	Panzertruppe-Pionierkompanie	Armored Combat Engineer Company
		Engineer Company (Armored Half-tracked Vehicles) of an Armored Engineer Battalion
	Sturmbootkompanie	Assault Boat Company
	Pionier-Radfahrerkompanie	Combat Engineer Bicycle Company
	Pioniernachrichtenzug (mot.)	Motorized Combat Engineer Signal Platoon
	Gebirgspionier - Nachrichtenzug bei Stäben (tmot.)	Mountain Combat Engineer Signal Platoon (Partly Motorized)
	Kavalleriepionierzug (mot.)	Motorized Combat Engineer Platoon (Cavalry)

Military Symbol	German	U. S. Equivalent
	Pionierwerkstattzug (mot.)	Motorized Combat Engineer Maintenance Platoon
	Brückenkolonne (Brüko) (mot.)	Motorized Bridging Column B
		Bridging Column T
	Leichte Pionierkolonne	Light Transport Column of Combat Engineers
	Leichte Pionierkolonne (mot.)	Motorized Light Transport Column of Combat Engineers
	Leichte Pionierkolonne (mot.)	Motorized Light Transport Column of Combat Engineers (in Panzer Division)
	Leichte Gebirgspionierkolonne (mot.)	Motorized Light Transport Column of Combat Mountain Engineers
	Kleine Pionierkolonne (mot.)	Motorized Light Transport Column of Combat Engineers
	Leicht zerlegbares Brückengerät	Sectional Bridging Equipment Unit
		Sectional Bridging Equipment Unit With Escort
	Herbert-Brückengerät	"Herbert" Ponton Bridging Equipment Unit

Military Symbol	German	U. S. Equivalent
		"Herbert" Ponton Bridging Equipment with Escort
	Schweres Schiffsbrückengerät	Heavy Boat Bridging Equipment Unit
		Heavy Boat Bridging Equipment Unit with Escort
	Brückengerätkolonne B	Equipment Unit for B Bridging Column
		Equipment Unit for B Bridging Column with Escort
	Kraftzug-Brückengerätkolonne B (mot.)	Tractor Echelon of a B Bridging Column
	Pioniergerätstaffel (mot.)	Motorized Engineer Tool Train

C. Groups:
  1. Example of a Diagrammatic Table of Organization:

Pionierbataillon (mot.) — Motorized Combat Engineer Battalion:
Headquarters
3 Motorized Engineer Companies each with 9 Light Machine guns
Motorized "B" Bridging Column
Motorized Light Transport Column of Combat Engineers

Military Symbol	German	U. S. Equivalent
2. Examples of Map Symbols:		
↑ ☐ 36	Pionierbataillon 36	36th Combat Engineer Battalion
⇐▭	Pionier-Marschkolonne	March Column of Combat Engineer Units

VIII. RAILWAY ENGINEER

A. Headquarters:

Military Symbol	German	U. S. Equivalent
	Stab eines Eisenbahnpionier-Regiments (mot.)	Motorized Railway Engineer Regimental Headquarters
	Stab eines Eisenbahnpionier-Bataillons (mot.)	Motorized Railway Engineer Battalion Headquarters
	Stab eines Eisenbahnpionier-Brückenbaubataillons (tmot.)	Partly Motorized Railway Engineer Bridge Building Battalion Headquarters
	Stab eines Eisenbahnpionier-Baubataillons	Railway Engineer Construction Battalion Headquarters

B. Units:

	Eisenbahnpionierkompanie (tmot.)	Partly Motorized Railway Engineer Company
	Eisenbahnpionierkompanie (mot.)	Motorized Railway Engineer Company.
	Eisenbahnpionier-Baukompanie	Railway Construction Company
	Eisenbahnpionier-Pfeilerbaukompanie	Pile Driver Company
	Eisenbahnfernsprechkompanie	Railway Telephone Operating Company

MILITARY SYMBOLS 49

Military Symbol	German	U. S. Equivalent
St.	Eisenbahn-Stellwerkkompanie	Railway Signals Company
W		Railway Engineer Water Supply Company
Feld	Feldbahnkompanie	Field Railway Company
Betr	Eisenbahnbetriebskompanie	Railway Operating Company
	Eisenbahn-Brückenbaukompanie	Company of a Railway Bridge Building Battalion
	Eisenbahnpionierpark	Depot Company of a Railway Bridge Building Battalion.
	Eisenbahnpionier-Baukompanie	Railway Engineer Construction Company
	Eisenbahn-Pionierparkkompanie	Railway Engineer Depot Company
	Pionierwerkstattzug	Engineer Railway Shop Platoon
Seil	Führer einer Seilbahnkompanie	Commander of a Cable Railway Company
Seil	Seilbahntrupp	Cable Railway Detachment
U S		Section Concerned With Underground Excavation (Foundations of Bridges, etc. on River Beds)

Military Symbol	German	U. S. Equivalent
	Eisenbahnpionierkolonne (mot.)	Motorized Railway Engineer Transport Column
	Eisenbahnbau-Pionierkolonne	Partly Motorized Column of a Railway Construction Battalion
	Eisenbahnpionierpark	Railway Engineer Supply Park
	Eisenbahnpionier-Brücke	Emergency Railway Bridge

IX. FORTRESS ENGINEER

A. Headquarters:

Military Symbol	German	U. S. Equivalent
F	Stab eines Festungspionierregiments	Fortress Engineer Regimental Headquarters
F	Stab eines Festungspionierbataillons	Fortress Engineer (Sector) Battalion Headquarters)
F	Stab eines Festungsbau-Pionierbataillons	Fortress Construction Battalion Headquarters

B. Units:

Military Symbol	German	U. S. Equivalent
F	Festungsbau-Pionierkompanie	Fortress Construction Company
F	Betonbaukompanie	Fortress Construction (Concrete) Company
F		Rock Drilling Company
F		Tunneling Company
F	Festungspioniertechnische Kompanie	Technical Company
F	Festungspionier-Parkkompanie	Fortress Engineer Depot Company
F	Festungspionier-Baukolonne (mot.)	Motorized Fortress Construction Transport Column
F	Festungsscheinwerferzug	Fortress Searchlight Platoon

Military Symbol	German	U. S. Equivalent
F ✡		Military Geological Section.
[Pi]	Festungspionierpark	Fortress Engineer Supply Park
Heim [Pi]		Fortress Engineer Supply Park (in Zone of Interior)

X. TECHNICAL
A. Headquarters:

Military Symbol	German	U. S. Equivalent
	Stab eines technischen Bataillons (mot.)	Motorized Technical Battalion Headquarters
		Motorized Technical Battalion (Gasoline "A") Headquarters
		Motorized Technical Battalion (Gasoline "B") Headquarters

B: Units:

		Motorized Technical Company (Electricity)
		Motorized Technical Company (Gas and Water)
		Motorized Technical Company (Mining, Excavation)
		Motorized Technical Company (Mining, "Cut and Cover" Construction)
		Motorized Technical Company (Gasoline "A")
		Motorized Technical Company (Gasoline "B")
		Motorized Technical Platoon (Gas and Water)

C. Example of a Diagrammatic Table of Organization:

Military Symbol	German	U. S. Equivalent
		Motorized Technical Battalion consisting of: Headquarters
		2 motorized Technical Companies (Electricity), each with 3 Light Machine Guns Motorized Technical Company (Gas and Water) with 3 Light Machine Guns.

XI. CONSTRUCTION

A. Headquarters:

Military Symbol	German	U. S. Equivalent
	Kommandeur der Bautruppen	Commander of Construction Units
	Stab eines Baubataillons	Construction Battalion Headquarters

B. Units:

	Baukompanie	Construction Company
	Betonbaukompanie	Construction (Concrete) Company
	Baukolonne	Construction Transport Column
	Baukolonne (mot.)	Motorized Construction Transport Column

55

XII. ROAD CONSTRUCTION

A. Headquarters:

Military Symbol	German	U. S. Equivalent
	Stab eines Strassenbaubataillons	Road Construction Battalion Headquarters
	Stab eines Radfahrer-Strassenbaubataillons	Road Construction Battalion (Bicycle) Headquarters

B. Units:

	Strassenbaukompanie	Road Construction Company
	Strassenbaukompanie (tmot.)	Road Construction Company (Partly Motorized)
	Radfahrer-Strassenbaukompanie	Bicycle Road Construction Company
		Partly Motorized Equipment Column of a Road Construction Battalion

XIII. SIGNALS

A. Headquarters:

Military Symbol	German	U. S. Equivalent
FÜ	Stab eines Führungsnachrichtenregiments (mot.)	General Headquarters Signal Regimental Headquarters (Motorized)
H.Gr.	Stab eines Heeresnachrichtenregiments (mot.)	Army Group Signal Regimental Headquarters (Motorized)
A	Stab eines Nachrichten-Aufklärungsregiments (mot.)	Signal Intelligence Regimental Headquarters (Motorized)
z.b.V	Stab eines Nachrichtenregiments, z. b. V. (mot.)	Signal Regimental Headquarters (Independent) (Motorized)
	Stab eines Panzer-Nachrichtenregiments	Panzer Army Signal Regimental Headquarters
	Stab eines Nachrichten-Horchregiments (mot.)	Signal Interception Regimental Headquarters (Motorized)
F	Festungsnachrichten-Kommandantur	Fortress Signal Regimental Headquarters
FÜ	Stab einer Führungsnachrichtenabteilung (mot.)	General Headquarters Signal Battalion Headquarters (Motorized)
H.Gr.	Stab einer Heeresnachrichtenabteilung (mot.)	Army Group Signal Battalion Headquarters (Motorized)

58 GERMAN MILITARY SYMBOLS

Military Symbol	German	U. S. Equivalent
A	Stab einer Armeenachrichtenabteilung (mot.)	Army Signal Battalion Headquarters (Motorized)
	Stab einer Nachrichtenabteilung	Signal Battalion Headquarters of an Armored Unit
K	Stab einer Korpsnachrichtenabteilung (mot.)	Corps Signal Battalion Headquarters (Motorized)
K	Stab einer Gebirgskorps-Nachrichtenabteilung (tmot.)	Mountain Corps Signal Battalion Headquarters (Partly Motorized)
Pz K	Stab einer Panzerkorps-Nachrichtenabteilung (mot.)	Panzer Corps Signal Battalion Headquarters (Motorized)
D or JD	Stab einer Infanteriedivisions-Nachrichtenabteilung (mot.)	Infantry Division Signal Battalion Headquarters (Motorized)
D	Stab einer Divisionsnachrichtenabteilung (tmot.)	Infantry Division Signal Battalion Headquarters (Partly Motorized)
D	Stab einer Panzerdivisions-Nachrichtenabteilung	Panzer Division Signal Battalion Headquarters
D	Stab einer Gebirgsdivisions-Nachrichtenabteilung (tmot.)	Mountain Division Signal Battalion Headquarters (Partly Motorized)
	Stab einer Horchnachrichtenabteilung (mot.)	Motorized Signal Interception Battalion Headquarters

MILITARY SYMBOLS

Military Symbol	German	U. S. Equivalent
		Field Exchange Unit Headquarters
F	Stab einer Festungsnachrichtenabteilung	Fortress Signal Battalion Headquarters
	Kompanieführer der Nachrichtentruppe	Signal Company Commander

B. Units:
  1. Signal:

Military Symbol	German	U. S. Equivalent
	Nachrichtenkompanie	Signal Company
	Nachrichtenkompanie (tmot.)	Signal Company (Partly Motorized)
Gr.	Grenznachrichtenkompanie (mot.)	Frontier (Guard) Signal Company (Motorized)
	Gebirgsnachrichtenkompanie (tmot.)	Mountain Signal Company (Partly Motorized)
Gr.	Grenzgebirgsnachrichtenkompanie (tmot.)	Mountain Frontier (Guard) Signal Company (Partly Motorized)
	Panzernachrichtenkompanie	Armored Signal Company
or	Leichte Nachrichtenkolonne (mot.)	Light Signal Transport Column (Motorized)
or	Leichte Gebirgsnachrichtenkolonne (mot.)	Light Mountain Signal Transport Column (Motorized)
		Armored Light Signal Transport Column (Motorized)

2. Telephone and Telegraph:

Military Symbol	German	U. S. Equivalent
	Fernsprechkompanie (tmot.)	Telephone Company (Partly Motorized)
	Fernsprechkompanie (mot.)	Telephone Company (Motorized)
	Gebirgsfernsprechkompanie (tmot.)	Mountain Telephone Company (Partly Motorized)
	Panzerfernsprechkompanie	Armored Telephone Company
	Fernsprechbaukompanie (mot.)	Telephone Construction Company (Motorized)
		Field Cable Company (Motorized)
		Motorized Cable Company (Higher Echelons)
		Telephone Installation Dismantling Company (Motorized)
	Fernsprechbetriebskompanie (mot.)	Telephone Operating Company (Motorized)
		Telegraph Construction and Operating Company (Motorized)
	Fernschreiberkompanie (mot.)	Teletype Company (Motorized)
	Fernsprechbaukompanie (mot.)	Line Building Company (Motorized)

Military Symbol	German	U. S. Equivalent
		Carrier Frequency Company (Motorized)
		Decimeter Wave Signal Company (Motorized)
		Motorized Screening and Reconnaissance Company
		Cable Detector Platoon

3. Radio:

	Funkkompanie (mot.)	Radio Company (Motorized)
or	Gebirgsfunkkompanie (tmot.)	Mountain Radio Company (Partly Motorized)
	Panzerfunkkompanie	Armored Radio Company
		Radio Beam (Direction Finding) Company (Motorized)

4. Interception:

	Horchkompanie (mot.)	Signal Intercept Company (Motorized)
	Nachrichten-Aufklärungskompanie	Signal Intelligence Company
	Nachrichten-Aufklärungstrupp (mot.)	Motorized Signal Intelligence Detachment
	Kleiner Horchstellentrupp	Radio Intercept Detachment
	Dolmetscherzug (mot.)	Interpreter Platoon (Motorized)

62 GERMAN MILITARY SYMBOLS

5. Miscellaneous:

Military Symbol	German	U. S. Equivalent
F		Fortress Cable Exchange Company
F	Festungskabelbauzug (mot.)	Fortress Cable Construction Platoon (Motorized)
F		Fortress Cable Burying Platoon
F	Festungsfunkzug	Fortress Radio Platoon
F	Festungs-Meldehund- und Brieftaubenzug	Fortress Messenger Dog and Carrier Pigeon Platoon
T		Pack Supply Column (Signals)
Vst	Verstärkerwagen (mot.)	Motorized Amplifying Unit (Electric)

6. Propaganda:

Prop	Propagandakompanie (mot.)	Propaganda Company (Motorized)
Prop	Propagandazug (mot.)	Propaganda Platoon (Motorized)

C. Installations:

K		Rear Area Signals Headquarters
FK	Feldnachrichtenkommandant	Field Signal Officer
N	Nachrichtenpark	Signal Equipment Depot

MILITARY SYMBOLS 63

Military Symbol	German	U. S. Equivalent
[N]	Feldnachrichtenpark	Field Signal Equipment Depot
↑[N]	Funk- und Fernsprechamt	Signal Office

D. Signal Sub-Units:

1. Telephone, Telegraph, and Teletype:

    a. Detachments:

⊥	Fernsprechgruppe (mot.)	Motorized Line Maintenance Squad
⊥l	Leichte Fernsprechgruppe (mot.)	Motorized Light Line Maintenance Squad
⊥s	Schwere Fernsprechgruppe (mot.)	Motorized Heavy Line Maintenance Squad
⊥	Leichter Fernsprechtrupp (mot.)	Motorized Light Telephone Line Maintenance Detachment
⊥	Mittlerer Fernsprechtrupp (mot.)	Motorized Medium Telephone Line Maintenance Detachment
⊥	Grosser Fernsprechtrupp (mot.)	Motorized Heavy Telephone Line Maintenance Detachment
⊥		Motorized Field Cable Detachment
⊥		Motorized Field Cable Detachment (Higher Echelons)
⊥	Fernsprechbautrupp (mot.)	Motorized Telephone Construction Detachment

64 GERMAN MILITARY SYMBOLS

Military Symbol	German	U. S. Equivalent
		Motorized Buried Cable Construction Detachment
	Fernsprechbetriebstrupp (mot.)	Motorized Telephone Operating Detachment
		Motorized Repeater Station Detachment
		Motorized Carrier Frequency Detachment
		Motorized Decimeter Wave Signal Detachment
		Motorized Decimeter Wave Balancing Detachment
		Motorized Teletype Installation Detachment
		Motorized Teletype Equipment Detachment
		Motorized Teletype Detachment
	Leichter Fernschreibertrupp (mot.)	Motorized Light Teletype Detachment
	Mittlerer Fernschreibertrupp (mot.)	Motorized Medium Teletype Detachment
	Schwerer Fernschreibertrupp (mot.)	Motorized Heavy Teletype Detachment
	Wechselstromtelegraphietrupp (mot.)	Alternating Current Telegraph Detachment (Motorized)

MILITARY SYMBOLS

Military Symbol	German	U. S. Equivalent
(symbol)		Cable Balancing Detachment (Motorized)
(symbol)		Cable Jointing Detachment (Motorized)
(symbol)		Cable Detector Detachment (Motorized)
(symbol)		Cable Burying Detachment (Motorized)

b. Stations:

●	Fernsprechstelle	Telephone Station
○	Fernsprechvermittlung	Telephone Exchange
8	Fernschreiberstelle	Teletype Exchange
∨		Repeater Station

c. Lines:

In line diagrams, the following colors are used:
- Green........ Infantry
- Red.......... Artillery
- Brown....... Divisional Signals
- Blue.......... Corps Signals
- Black........ Army and Army Group Signals

———	Einfachleitung	Single Wire Circuit
o———o	Feldkabeleinfachleitung	Field Cable Single Wire Circuit
—+++—	Doppelleitung	Two-Wire Circuit
o—+++—o	Feldkabeldoppelleitung	Field Cable Two-Wire Circuit
—//—//—		Field Long Distance Cable

GERMAN MILITARY SYMBOLS

Military Symbol	German	U. S. Equivalent
—•—•—		Field Permanent Line
—#—#—		Field Cable (Higher Echelons)
2F 1T —#—#—		Field Cable With 2 Telephones and 1 Teletype
10F 6T —ww—w†		Field Permanent Line With 10 Carrier Telephone and 6 Teletype Circuits
—•—3470—•—	Number Shown Denotes the Pair Number Received For the Army	⎧ Line Allocated From Civilian Post Office System ⎨ ⎩ Cable Allocated From Civilian Post Office System
∽∽∽∽∽ 3653-4070-4072		
∿∿∿∿∿		Decimeter Wave Circuit

2. Radio:

    a. Detachments:

	German	U. S. Equivalent
	Tornisterfunktrupp (mot.)	Portable Radio Detachment (Motorized)
	Leichter Funktrupp (mot.)	Light Radio Detachment (Motorized)
	Leichter Gebirgsfunktrupp (mot.)	Light Mountain Radio Detachment (Motorized)
	Mittlerer Funktrupp (mot.)	Medium Radio Detachment (Motorized)
	Schwerer Funktrupp (mot.)	Heavy Radio Detachment (Motorized)

MILITARY SYMBOLS 67

Military Symbol	German	U. S. Equivalent
	Schlüsseltrupp (mot.)	Cipher Detachment (Motorized)

    b. Stations:

	Funkstelle	Radio Station
30W (a)	Funkstelle mit 30 Watt Sender	30-Watt Radio Station
	Feste Funkstelle	Fixed Radio Station
	Sender	Transmitter
	Empfänger	Receiver

    c. Methods of Operation:

	Funklinie	Two-Station Net
	Sternverkehr	Directed Net
	Netzverkehr	Free Net

3. Interception:

    a. Detachments:

	Horchtrupp (mot.)	Radio Intercept Detachment (Motorized)
	Funkpeiltrupp (mot.)	Radio Beam (Direction Finding) Detachment (Motorized)

GERMAN MILITARY SYMBOLS

Military Symbol	German	U. S. Equivalent
		Radio Plotting Detachment (Motorized)
	Lauschtrupp (mot.)	Line Interception Detachment (Motorized)
	Horchtrupp (mot.)	Listening Detachment (Motorized)

b. Stations:

	Horchstelle; Empfänger	Listening Post; Receiving Set
	Horchstelle	Listening Station
	Feste Empfängerstelle	Fixed Receiving Station
	Peilstelle	Radio Beam (Direction Finding) Station
		Radio Plotting Station

4. Other Methods of Communication:

	Blinker	Blinker
	Blinkgerät (mot.)	Motorized Blinker Signal Equipment
	Blinkertrupp (mittel, klein)	Blinker Detachment (Medium, Small)
	Blinkverbindung	Blinker Connection Between Two Points
	Meldehundtrupp	Messenger Dog Detachment
	Meldehundverbindung	Messenger Dog Communication

MILITARY SYMBOLS 69

Military Symbol	German	U. S. Equivalent
⊥K		Photophone Detachment
⊢------⊣		Photophone Communication
▭	Feste Brieftaubenstelle	Fixed Carrier Pigeon Loft
▭	Brieftaubenstelle	Carrier Pigeon Loft
⌢	Abflugstelle	Carrier Pigeon Releasing Point
⌢.⌢.⌢	Heeresbrieftaubenverbindung	Carrier Pigeon Communication

5. Miscellaneous:

M.Kpf	Meldekopf	Advanced Message Center
M.S.St	Meldesammelstelle	Message Center
↑	Hochantenne	High Aerial
⌐→	Bodenantenne	Ground Aerial
⟁	Rahmenantenne	Frame Aerial
⊥	Erde	Ground

XIV. CHEMICAL

A. Headquarters:

Military Symbol	German	U. S. Equivalent
	Stab eines Nebelregiments (mot.)	Motorized Smoke (Chemical Warfare Service) Regimental Headquarters
	Stab einer Nebelabteilung (mot.)	Motorized Smoke (Chemical Warfare Service) Battalion Headquarters
Er	Stab einer Entgiftungsabteilung (mot.)	Motorized Decontamination Battalion Headquarters
Str Eg	Stab einer Strassen-Entgiftungsabteilung (mot.)	Motorized Road Decontamination Battalion Headquarters

B. Units:

	Nebelwerfertrupp (mot.)	Motorized Smoke-Laying (Chemical Warfare Service) Detachment (Type 35)
		Motorized Smoke Laying (Chemical Warfare Service) Detachment (Type 40) (Tractor-Drawn)
		Motorized Smoke Laying (Chemical Warfare Service) Detachment (Tractor-Drawn) (Type d)

MILITARY SYMBOLS 71

Military Symbol	German	U. S. Equivalent
		Motorized Smoke Laying (Chemical Warfare Service) Detachment (Tractor-Drawn)(Type e)
		Motorized Heavy Smoke Laying (Chemical Warfare Service) Detachment
	Engiftungskompanie (mot.)	Motorized Decontamination Company
	Gasspürerkompanie (mot.)	Motorized Gas Sentry Company (With Dogs)
Str	Strassen-Entgiftungskompanie (mot.)	Motorized Road Decontamination Company
	Leichte Nebelkolonne (mot.)	Motorized Smoke Laying Light Transport Column
	Leichte Entgiftungskolonne (mot.)	Motorized Decontamination Light Transport Column
		Motorized Decontamination Equipment Light Transport Column

C. Groups:

1. Example of a Diagramatic Table of Organization:

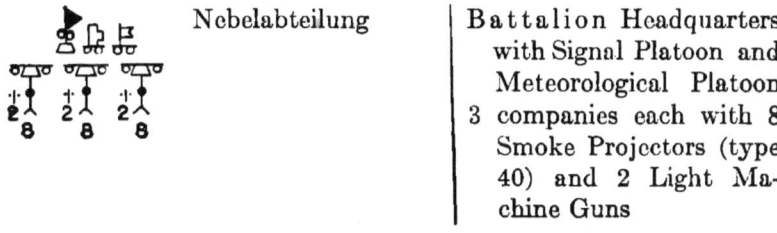

Nebelabteilung — Battalion Headquarters with Signal Platoon and Meteorological Platoon 3 companies each with 8 Smoke Projectors (type 40) and 2 Light Machine Guns

2. Examples of Map Symbols:

Military Symbol	German	U. S. Equivalent
⚑ II/51		2nd Battalion, 51st Smoke Regiment (Chemical Warfare Service)
⚑ 2		2nd Smoke Battalion (Independent) (Chemical Warfare Service)
🚗 104		104th Decontamination Battalion

XV. TRANSPORT
A. Headquarters:

Military Symbol	German	U. S. Equivalent
	Stab eines Kraftwagentransportregiments	Motor Transport Regimental Headquarters
	Stab einer Kraftfahrabteilung	Motor Transport Battalion Headquarters
	Stab einer Kraftfahrabteilung (tmot.)	Partly Motorized Transport Battalion Headquarters
	Stab einer Kraftfahrabteilung	Motor Transport Battalion Headquarters
		Motor Transport Battalion Headquarters on Self-propelled Mount
	Stab einer Kraftwagentransportabteilung	Motor Transport Battalion Headquarters (Troop Carrying)
	Führer einer Kraftfahrkompanie	Transport Company Commander
	Führer einer Kraftwagenkompanie	Motor Transport Company Commander

B. Units:

	Kraftfahrkompanie	Transport Company
	Kraftfahrkompanie (mot.)	Motor Transport Company
	Kraftwagentransportkompanie	Motor Transport Company (Troop Carrying)
		Motor Transport (Troop Carrying) Company

74　GERMAN MILITARY SYMBOLS

Military Symbol	German	U. S. Equivalent
		Motor Transport (Troop Carrying) Company (With Trailers)
		Ammunition Motor Transport Company (Half-track) on Self-propelled Mounts
	Fahrschwadron	Wagon Train
	Erkundungszug (mot.)	Motorized Reconnaissance Platoon (Motor Transport Battalion)
	Kraftfahrzug	Motor Transport (Troop Carrying) Platoon
	Kraftfahrzug	Motor Transport (Troop Carrying) Platoon (With Trailers)
	Kraftfahrpark	Motor Transport Park

C. Groups:

1. Example of a Diagramatic Table of Organization:

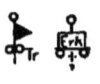

Motor Transport (Troop Carrying) Headquarters Consisting of:
Headquarters with Motorized Reconnaissance Platoon (with 1 Light Machine Gun)

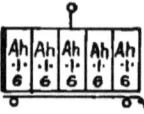

5 Motor Transport (Troop Carrying) Companies (With Trailers), Each With 6 Light Machine Guns

MILITARY SYMBOLS 75

2. Examples of Map Symbols:

Military Symbol	German	U. S. Equivalent
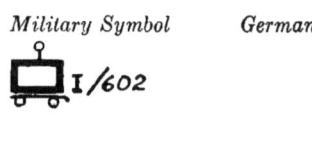		1st Battalion, 602nd Motor Transport (Troop Carrying) Regiment
⇐══════		Column of Partly Motorized Transport Units (on the March)

D. Trains of Combat Troops:

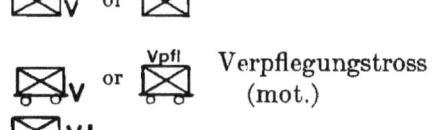 Verpflegungstross — Ration Train (Horse-drawn)

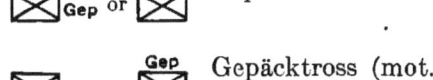 Verpflegungstross (mot.) — Motorized Ration Train

⊠VI — Ration Train (Horse-drawn), 1st Echelon

⊠ VII — Motorized Ration Train 2nd Echelon

 Gepäcktross — Baggage Train (Horse-drawn)

⊠Gep or ⊠Gep Gepäcktross (mot.) — Motorized Baggage Train

⊠Gef or ⊠Gef.Stff Gefechtsstaffel — Combat Train

If it is desired to show to which arm the train belongs, the basic sign of the arm must be added:

 Pioniergefechtsstaffel — Combat Engineer Combat Train

⊠Gef Panzergefechtsstaffel — Panzer Combat Train

XVI. SURVEY AND MAP PRINTING

A. Headquarters:

Military Symbol	German	U. S. Equivalent
		Motorized Survey and Map Reproduction Battalion Headquarters

B. Units:

Military Symbol	German	U. S. Equivalent
	Vermessungskompanie (mot.)	Motorized Survey Company
	Vermessungs-Stabskompanie (mot.)	Motorized Headquarters Company of a Motorized Survey Unit
	Druckereikompanie (mot.)	Motorized Printing Company
		Motorized Mapping Company
	Vermessungstrupp (mot.)	Motorized Survey Platoon
		Motorized Plotting Platoon
		Motorized Constructional Platoon
		Motorized Photographic Platoon
		Motorized Signal Platoon of a Motorized Survey Unit

Military Symbol	German	U. S. Equivalent
⌾		Motorized Maintenance Platoon of a Motorized Survey Unit
⌾	Druckereizug (mot.)	Motorized Printing Platoon
⌾A		Motorized Map Printing Office of an Army
⌾K		Motorized Map Printing Office of a Corps
⌾D		Motorized Map Printing Office of a Division
⌾Pz. D		Panzer Division Motorized Map Printing Office

C. Installations:

⌾		Motorized Army Map Depot
⌾		General Headquarters Map Depot

XVII. SERVICES

Color Scheme:
    Supply____ _____ Brown
    Administrative_____ Green
    Medical_____ Light Red
    Veterinary_____ Dark Red
    Postal_____ Yellow

A. Supply:

1. Headquarters:

Military Symbol	German	U. S. Equivalent
		Service of Supply Headquarters of a Panzer Army
	Stab eines Armeenachschubführers	Service of Supply Headquarters of an Army
Kdo. Pk		Headquarters, Army Parks
F	Stab eines Festungsnachschubführers	Fortress Service of Supply Headquarters
K	Stab eines Korpsnachschubführers	Motorized Corps Service of Supply Headquarters
	Stab des Quartiermeisters	Headquarters, Corps Service of Supply
	Rückwärtige Dienste Div. Stab	Headquarters, Division Rear Area Services

MILITARY SYMBOLS

Military Symbol	German	U. S. Equivalent
	Stab eines Nachschubführers	Headquarters of Service of Supply Commander (Horse)
	Stab eines Nachschubführers (mot.)	Headquarters of Service of Supply Commander (Motorized)
D or JD	Divisions-Nachschubführer	Headquarters, Service of Supply Commander in Infantry Division
D	Divisions-Nachschubführer (tmot.)	Division Service of Supply Headquarters (Partly Motorized)
D	Divisions-Nachschubführer (mot.)	Division Service of Supply Headquarters (Motorized)
		Panzer Division Service of Supply Headquarters
Kol.	Stab einer Fahrkolonne	Headquarters of Horse Supply Column
Kol.	Stab einer Kraftfahrkolonne (mot.)	Headquarters of Motorized Supply Column
Bg	Stab eines Gebirgsbrigadenachschubführers	Headquarters of Service of Supply Command in Mountain Brigade
T	Gebirgsträgernachschubführer	Mountain Pack Battalion Headquarters
Kfz. Inst		Motorized Motor Truck Repair Unit Headquarters

80 GERMAN MILITARY SYMBOLS

Military Symbol	German	U. S. Equivalent
	Stab eines Nachschubführers, z. b. V.	Supply Headquarters (Independent) (e. g., for Port Duties)

2. Units:

Military Symbol	German	U. S. Equivalent
	Nachschubkompanie	Service of Supply Company
	Nachschubkompanie (mot.)	Motorized Service of Supply Company
	Gebirgsnachschubkompanie	Mountain Service of Supply Company
	Gebirgsnachschubkompanie (mot.)	Motorized Mountain Service of Supply Company
Ers. 25		Spare Parts Echelon (25 Tons)
Ers. 50		Spare Parts Echelon (50 Tons)
®		Tire Echelon
® Jnst.		Tire Repair Echelon
	Tankstelle (mot.)	Motorized Filling Station
Verbl.		Motorized Ethylizing Section
		Gasoline Testing Section
		Snow Plow Section
	Leichte Fahrkolonne	Light Column (17 Tons)
	Fahrkolonne (30 T.)	Horse Transport Column (30 Tons)

Military Symbol	German	U. S. Equivalent
⊨	Fahrkolonne für Kavallerieverbände (30 T.)	Horse Transport Column for Cavalry Units (30 Tons)
⊴	Gebirgsfahrkolonne (15T.)	Horse Transport Column for Mountain Units (15 Tons)
≣	Grosse Fahrkolonne (60 T.)	Heavy Horse Transport Column (60 Tons)
○―○	Kleine Kraftwagenkolonne (30 T.)	Light Motor Transport Column (30 Tons)
Pz.Ers. ○―○		Motorized Tank Spare Parts Column
Bergung ○―○	Bergungskolonne	Motorized Salvage Column
▲T or ▲	Gebirgsträgerkompanie	Mountain Pack Company
M	Munitionskompanie (tmot.)	Partly Motorized Ammunition Company
Betr.St	Betriebsstoffkompanie (mot.)	Motorized Motor Fuel-Transport Company
☼	Werkstattkompanie (mot.)	Motorized Maintenance Company
Feld ☼	Feldwerkstattkompanie (mot.)	Motorized Field Maintenance Company
		Motorized Recovery Company
Kfz.Inst		Motorized Motor Truck Repair Company

82   GERMAN MILITARY SYMBOLS

Military Symbol	German	U. S. Equivalent
Kw or	Kraftwagenwerkstattzug (mot.)	Mobile Motor Repair Shop Platoon
Wm.	Waffenmeisterzug (mot.)	Motorized Ordnance Repair Platoon
Pz.Inst	Waffenmeisterzug (mot.)	Tank Repair Platoon
Zg. Kw. Jnst		Tractor Repair Platoon
		Rail Trolley Platoon
	Gasszug für den Gasschutz	Gas Protection Platoon
W	Wasserversorgungskolonne (mot.)	Motorized Water Transport Column
Pz.Ers.		Tank Spare Parts Echelon
	Grosse Kraftwagenkolonne (60 T.)	Heavy Motor Transport Column (60 Tons)
	Kleine Kraftwagenkolonne für Betriebsstoff (25 cbm)	Light Motor Transport Column for Fuel (25 Cubic Meters)
	Grosse Kraftwagenkolonne für Betriebsstoff (50 cbm)	Heavy Motor Transport Column for Fuel (50 Cubic Meters)

3. Installations:

J	Infanteriepark	Infantry Park
A	Artilleriepark	Artillery Park
G	Gasschutzgerätpark	Anti-Gas Equipment Park
PI	Pionierpark	Engineer Depot

Military Symbol	German	U. S. Equivalent
F [Pi]	Festungspionierpark	Fortress Engineer Equipment Depot
[N]	Nachrichtenpark	Signal Depot
[Kf.]	Kraftfahrpark	Motor Transport Park
H [Kf.]	Heeres-Kraftfahrpark	General Headquarters Motor Transport Equipment Depot
H [Kf.]	Heeres-Kraftfahrpark (tmot.)	Partly Motorized General Headquarters Motor Transport Equipment Depot
H [Kf.]	Heeres - Kraftfahrpark (mot.)	Motorized General Headquarters Motor Transport Equipment Depot
Heim [Kf.]	Heimats-Kraftfahrpark	Motor Transport Equipment Depot (in Zone of Interior)
[H]	Heergerätpark	Army Equipment Depot
Ers. [Z]		Central Spare Parts Depot
Ers [Pz.]		Tank Spare Parts Depot
[Gl.K]		Caterpillar Tracks Depot
Ers. [Zg.Kw]		Tractor Spare Parts Depot
Ers. [Pz.Sp.]		Armored-Car Spare Parts Depot
[⊛]		Tire Depot

GERMAN MILITARY SYMBOLS

Military Symbol	German	U. S. Equivalent
R+Ers		Tire and Spare Parts Depot
[symbol]		Supply Depot for Supplies Dropped by Air
M or Mun	Munitionslager der Armee	Ammunition Dump (in Forward Area)
U/M or U/Mun.	Umschlagstelle für Munition	Ammunition Transloading Point
A/M or A/Mun.	Ausgabestelle für Munition	Ammunition Distributing Point
H.MA or H.MA	Heeresmunitionsanstalt	Army Ammunition Loading Factory
M/S.St. or S.St./Mun.	Sammelstelle für Munition	Ammunition Collecting Dump
Ger./S.St. or S.St./Gerat	Sammelstelle für Gerät	Equipment Collecting Point
Beute/S.St.	Sammelstelle für Beute	Captured Equipment Salvage Depot
Gefang/S.St.	Sammelstelle für Gefangene	Prisoner of War Cage
[symbol]	Ortsfeste Tankstelle	Stationary Filling Station
[symbol]	Tankstelle für Einzelfahrzeuge (mot.)	Filling Station for Individual Vehicles (Motorized)
[symbol]		Gasoline Distributing Point
[symbol]	Eisenbahntankstelle	Railway Filling Station (Full)

MILITARY SYMBOLS 85

B. Administrative:
  1. Units:

Military Symbol	German	U. S. Equivalent
HZA	Heereszeugamt	Army Ordnance Department
A.Vpfl.A	Armeeverpflegungsamt	Army Ration Supply Office
AVA	Armeeverpflegungsamt (mot.)	Motorized Army Ration Supply Office
ABA	Armeebekleidungsamt (mot.)	Motorized Army Clothing Office
Vpfl.A	Divisionsverpflegungsamt	Divisional Supply Office
DVA	Divisionsverpflegungsamt (mot.)	Motorized Divisional Supply Office
VA z.b.V.	Verpflegungsamt, z.b.V.	Motorized Supply Office (Independent)
HVD	Heeresverpflegungsamt	Permanent Army Supply Office
HUV		Permanent Army Billeting Office
Nsch / Vpfl.A	Nachschubverpflegungsamt	Ration Supply Replacement Office
▨ or ⌀	Bäckereikompanie, nicht in Betrieb	Field Bakery Company (Not in Operation)
▨ or ⌀	Bäckereikompanie, nicht in Betrieb (mot.)	Motorized Field Bakery Company (Not in Operation)
⌀	Bäckereikompanie, in Betrieb	Field Bakery Company (in Operation)

GERMAN MILITARY SYMBOLS

Military Symbol	German	U. S. Equivalent
	Schlächtereikompanie (mot.)	Motorized Slaughter Company
		Railway Kitchen Company
		Clothing Repair Train
		Motorized Kitchen Company
or	Wirtschaftskompanie (tmot.)	Administrative Service Company (or Economic Functions Company) (Partly Motorized)
	Schlächtereizug, nicht in Betrieb	Slaughter Platoon (Not in Operation)
or	Schlächtereizug, nicht in Betrieb (mot.)	Motorized Slaughter Platoon (Not in Operation)
	Schlächtereizug, in Betrieb	Slaughter Platoon (in Operation)

2. Installations:

EVM		Depot Units Supply Depot
Vpfl. A or AVL	Armee-Verpflegungslager	Army Ration Supply Depot
KVL	Korps-Verpflegungslager	Corps Ration Supply Depot
Vpfl. D or DVL	Divisions-Verpflegungslager	Divisional Ration Supply Depot
ABL	Armee-Bekleidungslager	Army Clothing Depot

Military Symbol	German	U. S. Equivalent
[A] [A] Vpfl V	Verpflegungsausgabestelle	Ration Supply Distributing Point
[U] [U] Vpfl V	Verpflegungsumschlagstelle	Ration Supply Transloading Point
[S.ST] Rauhf.	Rauhafer-Sammelstelle	Green Fodder Collecting Depot
[Vieh]	Viehpark	Cattle Enclosure
[Vpfl.]	Verpflegungslager	Ration Supply Depot

C. Medical:

1. Headquarters:

	Stab einer Armeesanitätsabteilung (mot.)	Medical Unit Headquarters of Army (Motorized)
Lz	Stab einer Kriegslazarettabteilung (mot.)	Evacuation Zone Hospital Headquarters (Motorized)
Res.Lz.	Stab einer Reservelazarettabteilung	Motorized Reserve Hospital Battalion Headquarters
	Stab einer Krankentransportabteilung	Ambulance Battalion Headquarters
	Stab einer Krankentransportabteilung (mot.)	Motorized Ambulance Battalion Headquarters
Res.Lz.	Stab eines Reservelazaretts (mot.)	Motorized Reserve Hospital Unit Headquarters

2. Units:

Military Symbol	German	U. S. Equivalent
	Krankenwagenkompanie	Ambulance Company
	Krankenwagenkompanie (mot.)	Motorized Ambulance Company
	Sanitätskompanie	Medical Company
	Sanitätskompanie (mot.)	Motorized Medical Company
1/2	Sanitätshalbkompanie	Half Medical Company
	Gebirgssanitätskompanie (tmot.)	Partly Motorized Mountain Medical Company
	Entgiftungskompanie (mot.)	Motorized Personnel Decontamination Company
	Krankenkraftwagenzug	Motorized Ambulance Platoon
	Kriegslazarett	Communications Zone Hospital
	Leichtkrankenkriegslazarett	Communication Zone Hospital for Slightly Wounded
	Feldlazarett	Field Hospital
	Feldlazarett (mot.)	Motorized Field Hospital
	Heimatlazarett	Hospital in Zone of Interior

MILITARY SYMBOLS 89

Military Symbol	German	U. S. Equivalent
	Lazarettschiff	Hospital Ship
	Leichtkranken-Lazarettschiff	Hospital Ship for Slightly Wounded
	Lazarettzug, leer	Hospital Train (Empty)
	Leichtkrankenzug, belegt	Train for Slightly Wounded (Full)
	Gemischter Lazarettzug	Mixed Hospital Train
		Quarantine Train
	Sanitätspark	Medical Supply Depot
	Sanitätszweigpark	Branch Medical Supply Depot
	Sammelsanitätspark	Composite Medical Supply Depot
	Auf dem Marsch und in der Unterkunft:	*On the March or in Billets or Barracks:*
	Krankensammelpunkt	Collecting Point for Sick
	Krankensammelstelle	Collecting Point for Sick (Ambulance Unit)
	Ortskrankenstube	Dispensary Station
	Ortslazarett	Local Hospital

GERMAN MILITARY SYMBOLS

Military Symbol	German	U. S. Equivalent
	Im Gefecht:	*In Combat:*
⊕	Verwundetennest	First Aid Station
⊟	Truppenverbandplatz	Regimental Dressing Station
⊛	Wagenhalteplatz	Ambulance Station
△	Hauptverbandplatz	Main Dressing Station
○	Leichtverwundetensammelplatz	Collecting Station for Slightly Wounded
⊟ Eg.	Entgiftungsplatz	Personnel Decontamination Center

3. Miscellaneous:

⊟	Leichtkrankenkriegslazarett, eingesetzt	Communications Zone Hospital for Slightly Wounded, (in Operation)
⊟	Kriegslazarett, eingesetzt	Communications Zone Hospital (in Operation)
⊟ S or ⊟ S	Feldlazarett, als Seuchenlazarett eingerichtet, eingesetzt	Field Hospital for Contagious Disease, in Operation
⊟ Res. or ⊟ Res.	Reservelazarett, eingesetzt	Reserve Hospital, in Operation

D. Veterinary:

▣	Veterinärkompanie	Veterinary Company

MILITARY SYMBOLS

Military Symbol	German	U. S. Equivalent
	Gebirgsveterinärkompanie	Mountain Veterinary Company
	Pferdelazarett	Veterinary Hospital
	Heimatpferdelazarett	Veterinary Hospital in Zone of Interior
	Pferdepark	Horse Enclosure
	Armeepferdepark	Army Horse Enclosure
	Divisionspferdepark	Divisional Horse Enclosure
	Heimatpferdepark	Horse Enclosure in Zone of Interior
		Remount Supply Depot
	Veterinärpark	Veterinary Park
		Veterinary Park in Zone of Interior
		Veterinary Supply Park
	Hauptpferdepark	Main Veterinary Park
		Veterinary Examination Center
	L. Veterinärkolonne (mot.)	Light Veterinary Column (Motorized)
	Pferdetransportzug	Horse Transport Train

Military Symbol	German	U. S. Equivalent
Pf. Kr.	Pferdekrankenkraftwagen-kolonne (mot.)	Motorized Ambulance Column for Horses
	Pferdeverbandplatz (Gefecht)	Dressing Station for Horses (Combat)
	Pferdekrankensammelplatz (Gefecht)	Collecting Station for Sick and Wounded Horses (Combat)
	Pferdekrankensammelpunkt (Marsch und Unterkunft)	Collecting Point for Sick and Wounded Horses (On March and in Cantonment)
Beute		Captured Horses Collecting Point

E. Postal:

   1. Headquarters:

H		General Headquarters Field Postal Headquarters
A		Army Field Postal Headquarters

   2. Units:

A	Armee-Feldpostamt	Army Post Office
	Feldpostamt	Field Post Office
	Feldpostamt (Mot.)	Motorized Field Post Office

MILITARY SYMBOLS 93

F. Provost:

1. Headquarters:

Military Symbol	German	U. S. Equivalent
FK		Line of Communications Area Headquarters
KrK		Area Headquarters
OK or O.Kdtr	Ortskommandantur	Local Police Headquarters (For Town or District)
⚑⚑	Stab eines Feldgendarmeriebataillons (mot.)	Motorized Military Police Battalion Headquarters
⚑		Motorized Traffic Control Battalion Headquarters

2. Units:

Military Symbol	German	U. S. Equivalent
⌧	Feldgendarmerieschwadron (mot.)	Motorized Military Police Troop
⌿	Feldgendarmeriekompanie	Military Police Company
⌧		Motorized Traffic Control Company
Wa.	Wachkompanie	Guard Company
⌧	Feldgendarmerietrupp	Military Police Detachment
⌧	Feldgendarmerietrupp (mot.)	Motorized Military Police Detachment
G.FP		Field Security Police
FS.Abt		Special Field Unit
Ausk	Auskunftstelle	Information Office
Gef.S.St.	Gefangenensammellstelle	Prisoners' Collecting Point

XVIII. MISCELLANEOUS

A. Tactical Boundaries:

Military Symbol	German	U. S. Equivalent
▬▬▬•▬▬▬	Heeresgruppegrenze	Army Group Boundary
▬▬▬▬▬	Armeegrenze	Army Boundary
▬•• ▬••	Panzerarmeegrenze	Panzer Army Boundary
▬• ▬• ▬	Korpsgrenze	Corps Boundary
▬ ▬ ▬ ▬	Divisionsgrenze	Divisional Boundary
— ·· — ·· —	Regimentsgrenze	Regimental Boundary
— · — · —	Bataillons—usw. Grenze	Battalion (or Equivalent Unit) Boundary
— — — —	Kompanie—usw. Grenze	Company (or Equivalent Unit) Boundary
··········	Zielgrenze	Target Boundary
—+—+—	Aufklärungsgrenze	Limit of Reconnaissance
╱‾╲ ╱	Hauptkampflinie	Main Line of Resistance

B. Railroads and Transport:

W.T.Ltg.	Wehrmachttransportleitung	Armed Forces Movement Control
WVD	Wehrmachtverkehrsdirektion	Armed Forces Traffic Control
Bv.TO	Bevollmächtiger Transportoffizier	Chief Traffic Control Officer (in Army Group or Army Headquarters)

MILITARY SYMBOLS

Military Symbol	German	U. S. Equivalent
[B.G.O.]	Beauftragter Generalstabsoffizier	Specially-Assigned General Staff Officer
[T.O.]	Transportoffizier	Transportation Officer
[T.V.St.]	Transportverbindungsstab	Movement Liason Office
[Trsp.Kdtr]	Transportkommandantur	Movement Control Headquarters
[Avs/K.]	Ausladekommission	Unloading Commission
[Bhf.Kdtr]	Bahnhofs - Kommandantur	Railway Transport Office
[Bhf.O]	Bahnhofsoffizier	Railroad Station Office
[Hf.O] or [Haf.O]	Hafenoffizier	Port Officer
[Wl.St]	Weiterleitungsstelle	Forwarding Station
[FBD]	Feldeisenbahn - Direktorat	Field Railway Directorate
[FB] Betr.	Feldeisenbahn - Betriebsamt	Field Railway Operation Office
[FB] Masch	Feldeisenbahn-Maschinenamt	Field Railway Engineering Office
[FB] Werk	Feldeisenbahn-Werkstättenamt	Field Railway Maintenance Office
[FBD]/A	Armee - Feldeisenbahndirektorat	Army Railway Directorate
[FB] Betr /A	Armee - Feldeisenbahnbetriebsamt	Army Railway Operation Office
[FB] Masch /A	Armee - Feldeisenbahnmaschinenamt	Army Railway Shop Bureau

GERMAN MILITARY SYMBOLS

Military Symbol	German	U. S. Equivalent
[FB Werk / A]	Armee - Feldeisenbahnwerkstattenamt	Army Railway Maintenance Office
[F.W.St.A]		Field Waterways Units
[W.St.R.Kdo]		Waterways Clearance Headquarters
[M] or [Mun]	Munitionzug	Ammunition Train
[Vpfl]	Verpflegungszug	Ration Train
[Betr.St] or [Betr]	Betriebsstoffzug	Motor Fuel Train
[V]		Pack Train
[Mehl] or [Me]	Mehlzug	Flour Train
[Ha]	Haferzug	Oats Train
[Vieh]	Viehzug	Cattle Train
[train symbol]	Truppentransportzug (haltend)	Troop Train (Stationary)
[train symbol]	Truppentransportzug (in Fahrt)	Troop Train (On the Move)
[train symbol]	Leerzug (haltend)	Empty Train (Stationary)
[train symbol]	Leerzug (in Fahrt)	Empty Train (On the Move)
ULM ← [train] 7.I D 24 tögl.	Transportbewegung der 7. Infanteriedivision nach Gegend Ulmmit 24 Zügen täglich	7th Infantry Division Moving by Rail to Ulm (24 Trains a Day)

MILITARY SYMBOLS

Military Symbol	German	U. S. Equivalent
	in einem Raum abgestellte Vollzüge (72 Züge)	Area Containing 72 Loaded Trains
	Trink- und Tränkanlage	Drinking and Watering Place
S.Bhf	Sammelbahnhof	Railroad Collecting Point
Spandau	Ladebahnhof Spandau	Entraining Station (Spandau)
Bremen	Ausladebahnhof Bremen	Detraining Station (Bremen) (or Railhead)
NS A	Armee-Ausladebahnhof für Nachschub	Army Railhead
Nsch.Sl.Hf.	Nachschubsammelhafen	Supply Collection Port
NS A	Armee-Ausladehafen für Nachschub	Base Port
Stettin Nsch	Ausladehafen für Nachschub, Stettin	Supply Unloading Port, Stettin
U	Umschlaghafen	Reloading Port

C. Obstacles:

1. Mines:

✳	Tellermine	Tellermine (Plate Mine)
+	Tellermine gesprengt	Tellermine Destroyed
●	Schreckladung oder S-Mine	S-Mine or Booby-trap

98 GERMAN MILITARY SYMBOLS

Military Symbol	German	U. S. Equivalent
✹	Schreckladung oder S-Mine gesprengt	S-Mine or Booby-Trap Destroyed
⊤ ⊤	Tellerminen mit Brückenstangen	Tellermines With Pressure Bars
± ±		Emergency Tellermines Connected by Bars
▀▀ ▀	Schnelleingesetzte Schreckladung	Quickly-laid Booby-trap
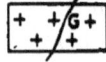		Tellermine Field (Buried: With Marked Lane)
		Mine Field (Laid on Surface: With Marked Lane)
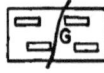		Mine Field With Pressure Plates (With Marked Lane)
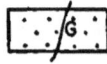		Anti-Personnel Mine Field (With Marked Lane)

2. Miscellaneous:

×××××××	Drahthindernis	Wire Entanglement
×××× ××××× ××××	Flächendrahthindernis	Wire Entanglements
✶-✶-✶	Maschendrahthindernis	Wire Mesh Obstacle
●-●-●	Stolperdraht	Trip Wire
∞∞∞∞∞	K– und S– Rollen	Concertina Wire
×××⚡×××	Starkstromsperre	High Tension Wire

MILITARY SYMBOLS 99

Military Symbol	German	U. S. Equivalent
⊕⋯⊖⊙	Zur Zerstorungvorbereitet	Prepared for Demolition
⊠⋯⊠ ⊠	Zerstört	Demolished
=⊚=	Leichte Baumsperre	Light Abatis (Tree Obstacle) (Prepared for Demolition)
=⊗=	Leichte Baumsperre, zerstört	Light Abatis (Demolished)
=⊚ˢ=	Schwere Baumsperre	Heavy Abatis (Prepared for Demolition)
=⊗ˢ=	Schwere Baumsperre, zerstört	Heavy Abatis (Demolished)
⬛⬛⊙⬛⬛▶	Eisenbahn, zur Zerstörung vorbereitet	Railway Line (Prepared for Demolition)
⬛⬛⊗⬛⬛▶	Eisenbahn, zerstört	Railway Line (Demolished)
⬛⬛┼⬛⬛	Eisenbahn-Grenzsperre	Railway Frontier Obstacle
○	Nachrichtenstelle, zur Zerstörung vorbereitet	Signals Installation (Prepared for Demolition)
⊗	Nachrichtenstelle, zerstört	Signals Installation (Demolished)
⊙→		Signals Installation (For Interruption in One Direction)
⊗→	Arrow denotes Direction of Interruption	Signals Installation (Interrupted in One Direction)
🬞🬞🬞		Glacis

GERMAN MILITARY SYMBOLS

Military Symbol / German	U. S. Equivalent
Barrikade aus Wagen, Steinen, Balken, u.s.w.	Barricade Made of Wagons, Stones, Earthworks, and Agricultural Implements
Barrikade mit Durchlass	Barricade With Passage for Own Traffic
Drahtseilsperre	Wire Cable Obstacle
	Obstacle of Steel Girders or Rails
Pfahlsperre	Picket Obstacle
Panzerwagengraben	Antitank Ditch
	(Close Country (Unsuitable for Tanks)
Abgeholzter Wald	Felled Trees, Cleared Forest
Niedergelegtes Gehöft	Farm Razed to the Ground
Anstauung (blaue Farbe)	Flooded Area (Colored Blue)
Stauanlage	Dam
	Gas Contaminated Area (Colored Yellow)
	Isolated Gas-Contaminated Areas (Colored Yellow)

MILITARY SYMBOLS 101

Military Symbol	German	U. S. Equivalent
		Area or Individual Feature Blocked Through Fire (Colored Red)
⚓	Zusetzen eines Durchlasses oder einer Brückenöffnung für Stauwerke	Block of a Sluice or Arch to Form a Dam
• • • •		Tank Obstacles (Blocks)
◆◆◆◆◆◆		Tank Obstacles (Pickets)
• • • • ·		Tank Obstacles (Drag Chains)
··•··•··•··		Tank Obstacles ("Hedgehogs")

(Also see "Defensive Positions", Page 102)

D. River Crossing:

1. Crossing Points:

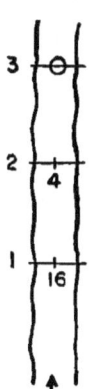

Crossing With 3 Large Floats

Crossing With 2 Ferries of 4-Ton Capacity

Crossing With 1 Ferry of 16-Ton Capacity

102 GERMAN MILITARY SYMBOLS

2. Bridges:

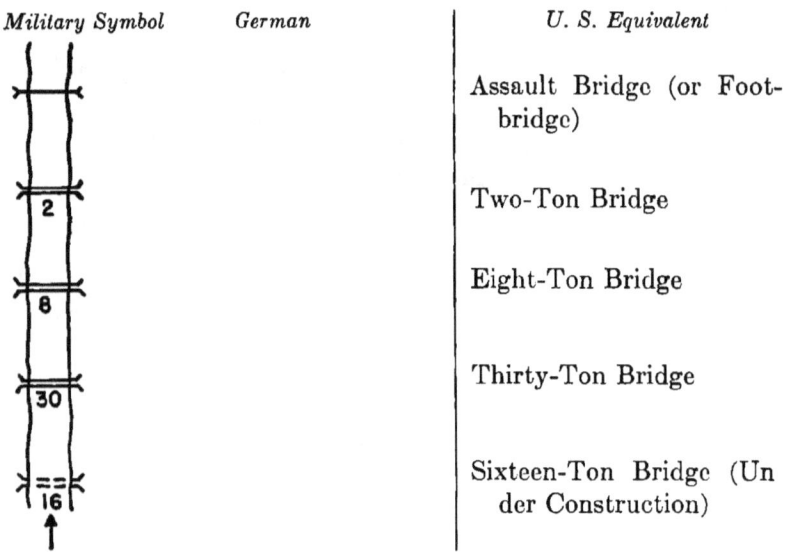

Military Symbol	German	U. S. Equivalent
		Assault Bridge (or Footbridge)
	2	Two-Ton Bridge
	8	Eight-Ton Bridge
	30	Thirty-Ton Bridge
	16	Sixteen-Ton Bridge (Under Construction)

E. Defensive Positions:

[....] Projected   ☐ Under Construction   ■ Completed

If fortified positions and battle headquarters are shown as command posts, the military symbol of the headquarters should be inserted.

✱ — Armored Casemate With Mechanical Installations

✱ P — Armored Casemate With Mechanical Installations and Antiaircraft Traversing Turret

✱ A — Armored Casemate With Mechanical Installations and Gun Traversing Turret

MILITARY SYMBOLS   103

Military Symbol	German	U. S. Equivalent
✱		Armored Casemate Without Mechanical Installations
✱J		Armored Casemate Without Mechanical Installations but With Infantry Observation Post
✱A		Armored Casemate Without Mechanical Installations but With Artillery Observation Post
✱N		Armored Casemate Without Mechanical Installations but With Signals Superstructure
◀▬		Machine Gun Pillbox (Casemate)
▶▬		Double Machine Gun Pillbox
◀▬▶		Double Machine Gun Pillbox (Dual Directional)
⊢▬⊣		Antitank Post
▶▬⊣		Machine Gun and Antitank Post
▬	Panzerwagengrube	Antitank Pit
⇐▬		Light Infantry Howitzer Position
●▬		Antiaircraft Artillery (88 mm) Position

GERMAN MILITARY SYMBOLS

Military Symbol	German	U. S. Equivalent
		Position With Light Howitzer in Turret
		Battle Headquarters or Dugout (Without Parapet)
		Battle Headquarters or Dugout (With Parapet)
A	Artilleriebeobachtungsstelle	Field Artillery Observation Post
		Field Artillery Observation Post (With Small Artillery Observation Tower)
J		Battle Headquarters For Infantry Observation (In Pillbox)
J		Battle Headquarters For Infantry Observation (In Pillbox with Loophole)
		Light-Signalling Post
N		Dugout for Signals (Main Exchange)
		Dugout with Radio
S		Storage Battery Charging Station
L.		Flash Spotting Post for Artillery
M		Ammunition Dugout
		Medical Dugout

MILITARY SYMBOLS 105

Military Symbol	German	U. S. Equivalent
		Elevated Machine Gun Post
		Elevated Artillery Observation Post
		Light Gun Emplacement
17 CM		Heavy Gun Emplacement
		Excavated Shelter (Tunneled or Roofed)
		Communication Trench
		Telephone Buried Cable
		Buried Cable (Bomb Proof)
		Buried Cable (Long Distance)
		Telephone Lines (Above Ground)
		Exchange (Cable Head)

(Also see "Obstacles", Page 97.)

F. Miscellaneous:

	German	U. S. Equivalent
	Ballonkompanie	Balloon Company
	Regimentsmusik	Regiment Bugle Corps
	Pferd	Horse
	Packpferd	Pack Horse

XIX. AIR

A. Higher Headquarters:

Military Symbol	German	U. S. Equivalent
	Oberbefehlshaber der Luftwaffe	Headquarters of Commander in Chief of the Air Force
	Kommandierender General der Luftwaffe	Headquarters of Commanding General of the Air Forces
	General der Luftwaffe beim Oberkommando der Heeres	Headquarters of General of the Air Force (for Cooperation With Army)
	Kommandur in einem Luftgau	Headquarters of a Commander of an Air District
		Antiaircraft Artillery Corps Headquarters
	Höherer Fliegerkommandeur	Headquarters of Higher Commander in the Air Force (Air Divisional Headquarters)
	General der Luftwaffe bei einer Armeegruppe	Air Force Commander With an Army Group ("KOLUFT") (The Letter of the Army Group is Added)
	General der Luftwaffe bei einer Armee	Air Force Commander With an Army ("KOLUFT") (The number of the Army is Added)

Military Symbol	German	U. S. Equivalent
	General der Luftwaffe bei einer Panzerarmee	Air Force Commander With a Panzer Army ("KOLUFT" Panzer Army)
		Fighter Commander's Headquarters With an Air Fleet
		Antiaircraft Artillery Brigade Headquarters

B. **Flying Corps:**

1. Headquarters:

	Stab Aufklärungsgeschwader	Reconnaissance Wing Headquarters
	Stab Kampfgeschwader	Bombardment Wing Headquarters
	Stab Sturzkampfgeschwader	Dive Bomber Wing Headquarters
	Stab Jagdgeschwader	Single-Engine Fighter Wing Headquarters
	Stab Zerstörergeschwader	Twin-Engine Fighter Wing Headquarters
	Stab Schlachtgeschwader	Ground Attack Wing Headquarters
		Mixed Reconnaissance Group Headquarters

Military Symbol	German	U. S. Equivalent
	Stab Fernaufklärungsgruppe	General Headquarters Long Range Reconnaissance Group Headquarters
	Stab Nahaufklärungsgruppe	Short Range Reconnaissance Group Headquarters
		Group Commander's Headquarters Attached to a Motorized Corps Headquarters
	Fliegerverbindungsoffizier	Air Force Liaison Officer at a Military Headquarters
	Stab Kampfgruppe	Bomber Group Headquarters
	Stab Sturzkampfgruppe	Dive Bomber Group Headquarters
	Stab leichter Jagdgruppe	Single Engine Fighter Group Headquarters
	Stab Zerstörergruppe	Twin Engine Fighter Group Headquarters
	Stab Schlachtgruppe	Ground Attack Group Headquarters

2. Units:

		Mixed Reconnaissance Group

MILITARY SYMBOLS

Military Symbol	German	U. S. Equivalent
	Fernaufklärungsgruppe	General Headquarters Long Range Reconnaissance Group
	Nahaufklärungsgruppe	Short Range Reconnaissance Group
		Army Reconnaissance Group Attached to a Motorized Corps
	Kampfgruppe	Bomber Group
	Sturzkampfgruppe	Dive Bomber Group
	Jagdgruppe	Single Engine Fighter Group
	Zerstörergruppe	Twin Engine Fighter Group
	Schlachtgruppe	Ground Attack Group
	Kampfstaffel	Bomber Squadron
	Sturzkampfstaffel	Dive Bomber Squadron
	Jagdstaffel	Single Engine Fighter Squadron
	Zerstörerstaffel	Twin Engine Fighter Squadron
	Schlachtstaffel	Ground Attack Squadron
	Aufklärungsstaffel (K)	Bomber Reconnaissance Squadron

GERMAN MILITARY SYMBOLS

Military Symbol	German	U. S. Equivalent
	Fernaufklärungsstaffel	General Headquarters Long Range Reconnaissance Squadron
	Fernaufklärungsstaffel	Long Range Reconnaissance Squadron
	Nahaufklärungsstaffel	Short Range Reconnaissance Squadron
		Army Co-operation Reconnaissance Squadron Attached to an Armored Formation
	Küstenfernaufklärungsstaffel	Long Range Coastal Reconnaissance Squadron
	Küstennahaufklärungstaffel (M)	Short Range Coastal Reconnaissance Squadron (Naval Force)
	Küstenmehrzweckestaffel (M)	Multi-Purpose Coastal Squadron (Naval Force)

C. Signals:

1. Headquarters:

 Stab Luftnachrichtenabteilung — Air Signal Battalion Headquarters (Army Cooperation)

2. Units:

 Luftnachrichtenabteilung — Air Signal Battalion (Army Cooperation)

 Air Signal Company With a Panzer Army

MILITARY SYMBOLS 111

Military Symbol	German	U. S. Equivalent
	Ln. Fernsprechbetriebskompanie	Air Signal Telephone Operating Company
	Ln. Fernsprechkompanie	Air Signal Telephone Company
	Ln. Funkkompanie	Air Signal Radio Company
	Luftnachrichtenflugmeldekompanie	Air Signal Aircraft Reporting Company

3. Permanent Signals Ground Organization:

	Flugmeldabteilung	Aircraft Reporting Battalion
(LV)		Terminal Exchange
(LW)		Central Exchange
(LDV)		Relay Exchange
	Flugwachkommando	Aircraft Observation Patrol
	Flugwache	Aircraft Sentry
	Flugmeldekommando	Aircraft Reporting Center
		Observer Section
		Flight Control Headquarters
		Flight Control Post

4. Miscellaneous:

	Luftnachrichtengerätkolonne	Air Signal Equipment Column

112 GERMAN MILITARY SYMBOLS

Military Symbol	German	U. S. Equivalent
	Luftfunkstelle	Air Force Radio Station
	Peilstelle	Radio Bearing (Direction Finding) Station

D. Antiaircraft Artillery:

1. Headquarters:

	German	U. S. Equivalent
	Höherer Kommandeur der Flakartillerie	Headquarters of Higher Echelons Antiaircraft Artillery (Divisional Sign. Not Yet Met With, but Logical)
	Stab Flakbrigade	Antiaircraft Artillery Brigade Headquarters
	Stab Flakregiment (oder Stab Flakgruppe)	Antiaircraft Artillery Regimental Headquarters
	Stab leichter Flakabteilung	Light Antiaircraft Artillery Battalion Headquarters
	Stab leichter Flakabteilung (mot.)	Light Antiaircraft Artillery Battalion Headquarters (Motorized)
		Light Antiaircraft Artillery Battalion Headquarters on Self-propelled Mounts
	Stab Flakabteilung oder Stab Flakuntergruppe	Antiaircraft Artillery Battalion Headquarters (a Mixed Battalion) (Also Used to Designate a Heavy Battalion, Which is Much Less Common)

Military Symbol	German	U. S. Equivalent
	Stab Flakabteilung (oder Stab Flakuntergruppe) (mot.)	Antiaircraft Artillery Battalion Headquarters (Motorized)
	Stab Eisenbahn-Flakabteilung	Reserve Railway Antiaircraft Artillery Battalion Headquarters
	Stab Ballonsperrabteilung	Ballon Barrage Battalion Headquarters
	Stab Flaktransportabteilung	Antiaircraft Transport Battalion Headquarters
	Stab Flakscheinwerferabteilung	Antiaircraft Searchlight Battalion Headquarters
	Stab Flakscheinwerferabteilung (mot.)	Antiaircraft Searchlight Battalion Headquarters (Motorized)

2. Units:

	Flakbatterie (2 cm) (mot.)	Motorized Antiaircraft Artillery Battery (20 mm)
	Flakbatterie (2 cm) auf Selbstfahrlafetten	Antiaircraft Artillery Battery (20 mm) on Self-Propelled Mounts
	Flakbatterie (3.7 cm) (mot.)	Motorized Antiaircraft Artillery Battery (37 mm)
	Flakbatterie (5 cm) (mot.)	Motorized Antiaircraft Artillery Battery (50 mm)

GERMAN MILITARY SYMBOLS

Military Symbol	German	U. S. Equivalent
	Flak-Stabsbatterie	Motorized Headquarters Company of a Motorized Antiaircraft Artillery Battery
	Luftsperrbatterie	Balloon Barrage Battery
	L. Flaktransportbatterie	Light Antiaircraft Artillery Transport Battery
	Flakscheinwerfertransportbatterie	Antiaircraft Searchlight Transport Battery
	Flakkolonne (22 Tonnen)	Light Antiaircraft Artillery Column (22 Tons Capacity)
	L. Flakkolonne (42 Tonnen)	Light Antiaircraft Artillery Column (42 Tons Capacity)
	Flakkolonne (48 Tonnen)	Antiaircraft Artillery Column (48 Tons Capacity)
	Flakscheinwerfertrupp (Vier 60 cm Scheinwerfer)	Antiaircraft Searchlight Section of 4 (600 mm) Searchlights
	Flakscheinwerfertrupp (Neun 150 cm Scheinwerfer) (mot.)	Antiaircraft Searchlight Section of 9 (1,500 mm) Searchlights (Motorized)
	Flaknachrichtenzug	Antiaircraft Signal Platoon

Military Symbol	German	U. S. Equivalent
⌀	Flakreserveeinheit	Reserve Antiaircraft Unit (A Diagonal Stroke Through the Circle at Base of all Antiaircraft Unit Signs Denotes "Reserve")
	Befehlsstelle einer Flakbatterie	Antiaircraft Artillery Battery Command Post
	Befehlsstelle eines Flakzuges	Antiaircraft Artillery Platoon Command Post

3. Weapons:

	Leichte Flak (2 cm)	Light Antiaircraft Gun (20 mm)
	Leichte Flak (2 cm) auf Selbstfahrlafette	Light Antiaircraft Gun (20 mm) on Self-Propelled Mount
		20-mm Antiaircraft Gun (4 Barreled)
	Leichte Flak (3.7 cm)	Light Antiaircraft Gun (37 mm)
		50-mm Antiaircraft Gun
	Schwere Flak (8.8 cm) (Pak/Flak)	Heavy Antiaircraft Gun (88 mm) (Multipurpose Gun Primarily for Antiaircraft)

116   GERMAN MILITARY SYMBOLS

Military Symbol	German	U. S. Equivalent
⊤	Schwere Flak (88 mm) (Pak/Flak) (mot.)	Heavy Antiaircraft Gun (88 mm) (Multipurpose Gun Primarily for Antiaircraft) (Motorized)
⊤	(See "Addenda", Page 143)	Heavy Antiaircraft Gun (105 mm)

E. Parachute Units:

   Stab einer Fallschirmjägerabteilung   Parachute Rifle Battalion Headquarters

   Fallschirmjägerkompanie   Parachute Rifle Company

F. Air Bases:

   Fliegerhorst   Permanent Air Force Station

   Seefliegerhorst   Naval Air Base

   Ziviler Flughafen   Civilian Airport

      Operational Airdrome, 1st Class

      Operational Airdrome, 2d Class

      Airdrome

      Prepared Airdrome

      Dummy Airdrome

      Advanced Landing Field

Alternative Landing Field

APPENDIX I

GROUND PANEL SIGNALS USED BY TROOPS FOR AIR COMMUNICATION

Military Symbol	German	U. S. Equivalent
✝	Hauptquartier	Headquarters
✢	Abwurfstelle	Message-Dropping Point
Y	Nicht verstanden	Do Not Understand
V	Wir verstehen, ja	Understand (Can Also Mean "Yes")
B	Feind bereitet Angriff vor	Enemy Preparing Attack
⊓	Feind greift an	Enemy is Attacking
|||	Stellung ist verlorengegangen	Position is Lost
╱⁻⁻	Feind links eingedrungen	Enemy Has Penetrated on Our Left
⁻⁻╲	Feind rechts eingedrungen	Enemy Has Penetrated on Our Right
⋁	Kampffront	Front Line
▽	Nein	No
☐	Wir sind eingeschlossen	We Are Surrounded
⊔	Unterstützung notwendig	Support Needed

GERMAN MILITARY SYMBOLS

Military Symbol	German	U. S. Equivalent
⊢o	Feindlicher Anklammerungspunkt	Center of Enemy Resistance
	oder	or
T	Feindlicher Anklammerungspunkt	Center of Enemy Resistance (Vertical Line Points Towards It)
‖⊢o	Feindliche Batterien	Enemy Batteries
N	Feindlicher Angriff zurückgeschlagen	Enemy Attack Repulsed
— — —	Wir halten die Linie.	We Are Holding the Line
⊓	Munition nötig	Ammunition Needed (Rifle, Machine Gun, Pistol, Antitank Rifle, Hand Grenade)
⊓	1. Mörsermunition nötig	Light Mortar Ammunition Needed
⊞	s. Mörsermunition nötig	Heavy Mortar Ammunition Needed
⊞	Artilleriemunition nötig	Artillery (75 mm) Ammunition Needed
⊞	Nebelgranaten nötig	Smoke Bombs Needed (105 mm)
⊞	Pakmunition nötig	Antitank Ammunition (37 mm) Needed
⊓⊓	20 mm Munition nötig	20-mm Ammunition Needed
⊢⊣	Lebensmittelvorräte nötig	Food Supplies Needed
↗	Wir gehen vor	We Advance (Are Ready to Attack)

MILITARY SYMBOLS

Military Symbol	German	U. S. Equivalent
VVV	Kein Feind	No Enemy
∧	Feindlicher Widerstand	Enemy Resistance (Pointer Indicates Situation of Enemy)
⫽F⫽	Feindlicher Widerstand, 1200 Meter	Enemy Resistance at 1,200 Meters
⫽F⫽	Feindlicher Widerstand, 1300 Meter	Enemy Resistance at 1,300 Meters
X X	Abwurfstelle für Vorräte	Point for Dropping Supplies
⊥	Abwurfplatz für Divisionsstab	Dropping Spot for Divisional Command Post
▽	Abwurfplatz für Regimentsstab	Dropping Spot for Regimental Command Post
=	Abwurfplatz für Bataillonsstab	Dropping Spot for Battalion Command Post
⩓	Äusserste Not	Extreme Emergency! (Only on Order of Battalion or Higher Command)
⫿⫿⫿	Medizinische Vorräte dringend nötig	Medical Supplies Urgently Required
T	Brennstoff nötig	Motor Fuel Needed (Yellow Stripe)
⫽	Funkausrüstung nötig	Radio Equipment Needed (Apparatus Destroyed)
⌐⌐	Landungsmöglichkeit	Possibility of Landing Here
⟋⟍	Keine Landungsmöglichkeit	No Place for Landing

APPENDIX II

NON-OFFICIAL AUXILIARY SIGNS

In addition to the foregoing military symbols, there exists a number of non-official, auxiliary signs. These representations may be found in training manuals and instruction books by independent authors, in military encyclopedias, in tactical books by military writers, and in some German Army Regulations where the symbols are not designated as "tactical."

Since the designers of these auxiliary signs worked independently, it follows that there can be no uniformity to the following series. It will be noted that two and sometimes three signs are given for one subject, and even this does not exhaust the possibilities.

No attempt has been made to compile an extensive list of these auxiliary signs. Only those most frequently encountered are given here.

A. Personnel

Military Symbol	German	U. S. Equivalent
	Kompanieführer	Company Commander
	Komp-Truppführer	Leader of Company Headquarters Detachment About Size of Squad
	Zugführer	Platoon Leader
	Zugtruppführer	Leader of Platoon Headquarters Detachment About Size of Half-Squad

MILITARY SYMBOLS 121

Military Symbol	German	U. S. Equivalent
●	Gruppenführer; Geschützführer	Squad Leader; Gun Corporal
⊖ ⊖	Truppführer (Stellv. Gr. F.)	Assistant Squad Leader
●	Truppführer l. Gr. W.	Leader of Light Mortar Section
●P	Führer des Pz. B. Trupp	Leader of Antitank Rifle Section
●F	Fernsprechtruppführer	Leader of Telephone Operating Detachment
⊙	Führer des Gefechtstrosses (auf Rad)	Leader of Combat Train (on Bicycle)
⊛ ⊙R	Rechnungsführer	Pay Sergeant
⊙ ▯ ▯	Oberfeldwebel (auf Rad)	Master Sergeant
⊙S	Schirrmeister	First Sergeant (Supply)
○	Gewehrschütze	Rifleman
⊕	Schütze 1 in Pz. B. Trupp	#1 Gunner in Antitank Rifle Section
○P	Schütze 2 in Pz. B. Trupp	#2 Gunner in Antitank Rifle Section
⊖	Schütze 1 beim l. Gr. W. Trupp	#1 Gunner with Light Mortar Section
⊖2	Schütze 2 beim L. Gr. W. Trupp	#2 Gunner (in Charge of Loading) With Light Mortar Section
⊕	1. M. G. Schütze 1 (Richtschütze)	1# Gunner on Light Machine Gun

122 GERMAN MILITARY SYMBOLS

Military Symbol	German	U. S. Equivalent
Ö	l. M. G. Schützen 2 – 4	#2 – 4 Gunner on Light Machine Gun
⬤	Richtschütze	Gunner
⊕ or ⬤	Sanitätsunteroffizier	Medical Non-Commissioned Officer
⊗ San	San. Uffz. (auf Fahrrad)	Medical Non-Commissioned Officer (on Bicycle)
[Pf] ○ Pf. or ⬤	Pferdewärter	Horse Holder
⊗ Pf.	Pferdewärter (auf Fahrrad)	Horse Holder (on Bicycle)
Ⓦ ⬤ ○ W	Waffen- und Geräts-Uffz.	Weapons and Instrument Non-Commissioned Officer
Ⓕ [ ] △	Fahrer	Driver
○ N ○ N	Uffz. für Nachrichtendienst	Signal Non-Commissioned Officer
○ Fe	Fernsprecher	Telephone Operator
○ F2	Fernsprecher 2	Telephone Operator #2
⊖ [ ] ○ M	Entfernungsmessmann	Range Finder Operator
⊗	Scherenfernrohrträger	Battery Commander's Telescope Carrier
○ M	Munitionsschütze	Assistant Gunner (in Charge of Loading)
○ ME	Messmann	Surveyor

Military Symbol	German	U. S. Equivalent
○ WE	Wettermann	Meteorologist
◎	Melder beim Komp.-Trupp	Company Messenger
⊙	Melder beim Zugtrupp	Platoon Runner or Orderly
♂	Spielmann beim Komp.-Trupp	Company Bugler
♂	Spielmann beim Zugtrupp	Platoon Bugler
○W Ⓦ	Waffenmeistergehilfe	Assistant Armorer
○H Ⓗ	Handwerker	Artisan
Ⓚ ○K	Koch	Cook
○V	Verpflegungsmann	Ration Man
⊕ Ⓚ	Krankenträger	Stretcher Bearer

B. Vehicles:

↕	Krad (Kraftrad)	Motorcycle
	s. Krad mit Beiwagen	Heavy Motorcycle with Sidecar
	gl. Pkw. mit Zugvorrichtung	Cross Country Personnel Carrier With Towing Device
	gl. Pkw. mit Pak	Cross Country Personnel Carrier With Antitank Gun

GERMAN MILITARY SYMBOLS

Military Symbol	German	U. S. Equivalent
	gl. Pkw. mit Mun.-Anhänger	Cross Country Personnel Carrier With Munitions Trailer
	Feldküche	Field Kitchen

SECTION III

Copies of German Maps and Tables of Organization

The purpose of this section is to acquaint intelligence personnel with the form used by the Germans in publishing their maps and tables of organization and to provide the intelligence personnel with an opportunity to practice interpreting them.

Geschwindigkeitstabelle

Marschgeschw in Std/Km	10	15	20	25	30	35	40	45	50	55	60	65	70	75
Fahrstrecke in Km	Minuten													
10	60	40	30	24	20	17,2	15	13,4	12	10,9	10	9,2	8,7	8
15	90	60	45	36	30	26,0	22,5	20,0	18	16,5	15	14,0	13,0	12
20	120	80	60	48	40	34,5	30	27,0	24	22,0	20	18,5	17,5	16
25	150	100	75	60	50	43,0	37,5	33,5	30	27,5	25	23,5	21,5	20
30	180	120	90	72	60	51,5	45	40,0	36	33,0	30	28,0	26	24
35	210	140	105	84	70	60,0	52,5	47,0	42	38,5	35	32,5	30	28
40	240	160	120	96	80	69,0	60	53,0	48	44,0	40	37,0	34	32
45	270	180	135	108	90	77,0	67,5	60,0	54	49	45	42	39	36
50	300	200	150	120	100	86,0	75	67,0	60	55	50	46	43	40
55	330	220	165	132	110	94,0	82,5	73,0	66	60	55	51	47	44
60	360	240	180	144	120	103,0	90	80,0	72	65	60	55	52	48
65	390	260	195	156	130	111,0	97,5	87,0	78	71	65	60	56	52
70	420	280	210	168	140	120,0	105	93,0	84	76	70	65	60	56
75	450	300	225	180	150	129,0	112,5	100,0	90	82	75	69	65	60
80	480	320	240	192	160	137,0	120	107,0	95	87	80	74	70	64
85	510	340	255	204	170	146,0	127,5	113,0	102	93	85	78	74	68
90	540	360	270	216	180	154,0	135	120,0	108	98	90	83	78	72
95	570	380	285	228	190	163,0	142,5	127,0	114	104	95	88	82	76
100	600	400	300	240	200	172,0	150	134,0	120	109	100	92	87	80

Erläuterungen zur Marschlängenübersicht.

Die Angaben über Längen und Zeiten der nachfolgend aufgeführten Einheiten bilden einen <u>Anhalt</u> für die Marschlängen beim Fahren und Halten. Hierbei sind bereits marschtechnische Einflüsse, Verbands- und Einheitsabstände und zur Regelung des Marsches ein= gesetzte Fahrzeuge berücksichtigt.

Die Einheiten der Jnf.-Div. (mot) gleichen vielfach denen der Pz.-Div., sodaß nur die hiervon abweichenden Einheiten aufgeführt sind.

<u>Als Abstand ist berechnet:</u> Jm Fahren Tachoabstand, mindestens aber 2o m, im Halten 4 u. 2o m.

<u>Als Abstand zwischen den Einheiten:</u> Jm Fahren 5o m, bei Geschwin= digkeiten über 5o km/Std., Tachoabstand, im Halten 25 m.

<u>Als Abstand zwischen den Verbänden:</u> Jm Fahren 25o m, im Halten 15o m.

Bei Nebel, Staub, Dunkelheit und unübersichtlichen Wegen verringern sich die Geschwindigkeiten und Fahrzeugabstände erheblich. Diese Einflüsse, sowie die jeweiligen Kampfverluste und Marschausfälle müssen in jedem einzelnen Fall bei Benutzung der Tabelle berücksich= tigt werden.

Marschlängen im Divisionsverband

Ges. Pz. Div. auf geschlossenem Marsch in 5 Marschgn mit 20 Min. Abstand zwischen den Marschgr.		
Bei 10 Km/Std.	Bei 25 Km/Std.	Im Halten mit 20m Fahrzeugabstand
120 Km 12 Std.	170 Km 7 Std.	120 Km

Fechtende Truppe einer Pz. Div. auf dem Marsch in 4 Marschgn mit 20 Min. Abstand zwischen den Marschgr. (ohne Sicherungsabstände)		
Bei 10 Km/Std.	Bei 25 Km/Std.	Im Halten mit 20m Fahrzeugabstand
90 Km 9 Std.	130 Km 5 Std.	90 Km

Ges. Inf. Div. (mot.) auf geschlossenem Marsch in 5 Marschgn mit 20 Min. Abstand zwischen den Marschgn		
Bei 10 Km/Std.	Bei 25 Km/Std.	Im Halten mit 20m Fahrzeugabstand.
90 Km 9 Std.	150 Km 6 Std.	90 Km

Fechtende Truppe einer Inf. Div. (mot.) auf dem Marsch in 4 Marschgr. mit 20 Min. Abstand zwischen den Marschgn (ohne Sicherungsabstände)		
Bei 10 Km/Std.	Bei 25 Km/Std.	Im Halten mit 20m Fahrzeugabstand.
70 Km 7 Std.	110 Km 4½ Std.	70 Km

Erläuterung zur Pz.-Div. und (mot.) I.Div.

Die Gesamtlängen der Pz.-Div. sowie der Inf.-Div.(mot) ergeben sich unter Berücksichtigung dessen, daß die gesamte Div. auf einer Straße einen längeren Marsch zurückzulegen hat. Es sind daher auch die rückwärtigen Dienste, sowie Gef.Tr.II und Kolonnen mit eingerechnet. Nicht eingerechnet sind Feldgend., sowie 10 % aller Fhrzg., die für Erkundung, Melde- und Absperrdienst eingesetzt sind.

Die fechtende Truppe der Pz.-Div. und Inf.-Div.(mot) ist hier noch ohne taktische Abstände berechnet. Um die Marschlängen der Div. in Vormarsch mit Sich.-Abst. zu erhalten, müssen die jeweiligen Marschgr.-Abstände, sowie die Anzahl der bereits eingesetzten Truppen (A.A., Flak usw.) berücksichtigt werden.

Für Melde-, Erkundungs- u. Absperrdienst, sowie durch Weglassen des Gef.Tr.II und der Kolonnen sind die Einheiten um 20 % verkürzt.

GERMAN MILITARY SYMBOLS

Marschlängen der Truppenteile einer Panzerdivision

Einheit	In Haufen und am Anf. m	In Haufen mit 20m Abstand u. bei 10km/Std m	In Haufen Min	Im Fahren mit 25 Km/Std m	Min	Einheit	Im ... m	Im Haufen mit 20m Abstand u. bei 10km/Std m	Min	Im Fahren mit 25 Km/Std m	Min	Einheit	In ... m	In Haufen mit 20m Abstand u. bei 10km/Std m	Min	Im Fahren mit 25 Km/Std m	Min
Div. Stb.	550	1800	11	2400	6	Schtz. Brig	14000	35000	210	46000	110	Nachr. Abt.	1000	3000	18	4000	10
Feldgend. Tr.	200	700	4,5	1000	2,5	Schtz. Brig. Stb.	150	250	2,5	400	1	Funk - Kp	400	1700	6,5	1400	3,5
						Schtz. Rgt.	5600	13000	80	18000	45	Fernspr. - Kp	400	1100	6,5	1400	3,5
Pz. Rgt. (3Abt)	6000	19000	115	26000	60	Schtz. Rgt Stb	500	1500	9	2000	5	l. Nachr. Kol.	150	350	2	400	1
Pz. Rgt. Stb	240	800	5	1000	2,5	Schtz. Btl.	2400	5000	30	7500	18						
Pz. Abt.	2000	5500	33	8000	20	Schtz. Btl. Stb.	200	400	2,5	500	1,2	l. Flak. Abt	1500	4700	28	6500	15
Pz. Abt. Stb.	200	450	2,5	600	1,5	Schtz. Kp.	400	1000	6	1300	3	2 cm Battr.	400	1200	7	1700	4
Pz. Abt Stb Kp	400	1100	6,5	1500	3,5	sthw. Kp	450	1100	7	1400	3,5	3,7 cm Battr.	300	1100	6,5	1500	3,5
l. Pz. Kp	350	1000	6	1300	3	M.G.Kp	450	1100	7	1400	3,5	l. Flak. Kol.	150	350	2,5	500	1,2
mittl. Pz. Kp.	350	1000	6	1300	3	l. Inf. Kol.	200	450	2,5	600	1,5						
Werkst Kp	500	1500	9	2000	5							Vers. Truppen	3500	16000	100	19000	50
l. Pz. Kol	150	450	2,5	600	1,5	Kradschtz. Btl	2200	7300	45	10000	20	Stb. Div Nachsch. Fhr.	150	400	2,5	600	1,5
						Kradschtz. Kp.	400	1300	8	1800	4,5						
Art. Rgt	5400	13000	80	19000	45	Krad. M.G. Kp	450	1500	9	2100	5	Nachsch Dienste	3400	10300	60	12800	30
Art. Rgt Stb	150	350	2	500	1,2							Kl. Kw. Kol	100	350	2	400	1
Pz. B. Battr.	700	1700	10	2100	5,5	Aufkl. Abt	1800	4300	26	7300	12	gr. Kw. Kol	200	700	4	800	2
l. Art. Abt	1400	3200	20	4800	12	Pz. Späh. Kp.	300	900	5,5	1300	3	Nachsch Kp.	200	600	3,5	700	2
l. Battr.	350	900	5,5	1100	3	l. a. a. Kol	150	400	2,5	600	1,5	Feldpostamt	50	700	1	150	0,4
s. Art. Abt.	1600	3700	22	5000	12							San. Dienste	1000	3000	18	4000	10
s. Battr.	350	1000	6	1300	3	Pi. Btl.	2300	5800	35	8300	20	Kr. Kw. Zg.	100	400	2,5	600	1,5
l. Art. Kol.	200	500	3	700	2	Pz. Pi. Kp	400	1000	5,5	1400	3,5	San. Kp.	250	650	4	1000	2,5
						Pi. Kp.	350	900	5,5	1300	3	Verw Dienste	450	1100	6,5	1300	4,5
Pz. Jäg. Abt.	1500	4200	25	6200	15	Brücko B.	350	900	5,5	1200	3	Verpfl Amt	100	300	1	400	1
Pz. Jäg. Kp.	300	900	5,5	1300	3	Brücko K	350	900	5,5	1200	3	Bäckerei- Kp	150	400	2,5	600	1,5
2cm Kp.	250	1000	6	1500	3,5	l. Pi. Kol	150	450	2,5	600	1,5	Schlacht. Zg.	100	200	1	350	1

Gen. Kdo. mit Korps-Tr. — Heerestruppen — J. D. (mot.) (nicht aufgeführte Einheiten siehe oben)

Einheit	m	m	Min	m	Min	Einheit	m	m	Min	m	Min	Einheit	m	m	Min	m	Min
Stb Gen Kdo	800	2000	12	3000	7,5	M.G Btl	1800	3700	22	5000	12	Inf. Rgt. (mot.)	5000	18000	100	22000	55
Staffel Kom Gen.	710	200	12	300	1	gem Flak Abt	2300	6500	40	8500	20	Inf Btl (mot.)	1400	4000	25	5600	14
1. St. Fhr Abt	250	600	3,5	750	2	Arko	60	150	1	200	0,5	J.G Kp (mot)	250	1100	6,5	1700	3
2. St Fhr Abt.	250	600	3,5	750	2	Brücken Bau- Btl (mot)	1200	6300	30	4500	10	Aufkl Abt	1500	3700	19	6300	15
Pz K Nachr. Abt	1500	4300	26	6000	15	Regt Nebelw d	5000	14000	85	17000	40	Pz. Jäg. Abt.	1700	3300	20	4500	13
K Nachsch Abt	800	2200	13	3000	7,5	Nebelw Abt	1400	3500	21	4400	11	Vers Truppen	4700	10000	60	18000	45
K. Werkst Zg	100	170	1	230	0,5	Entgift. Abt	1800	5000	30	6200	15	Nachsch Dienste	2500	7600	45	9500	22
Feldgend Tr. (bevett)	300	700	4	900	2							San Dienste	1200	3800	23	5000	10
Feldgend Tr (mit Obst.)	250	500	3	700	2							Feldlaz. (mot)	170	450	2,5	600	1,5

DOCUMENTS 129

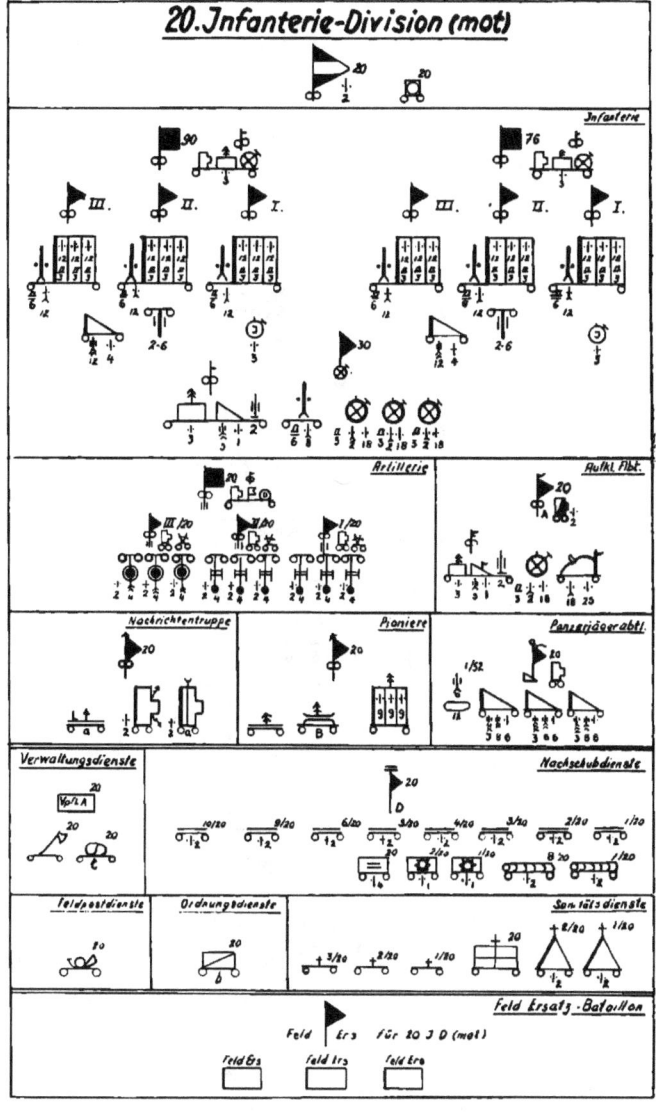

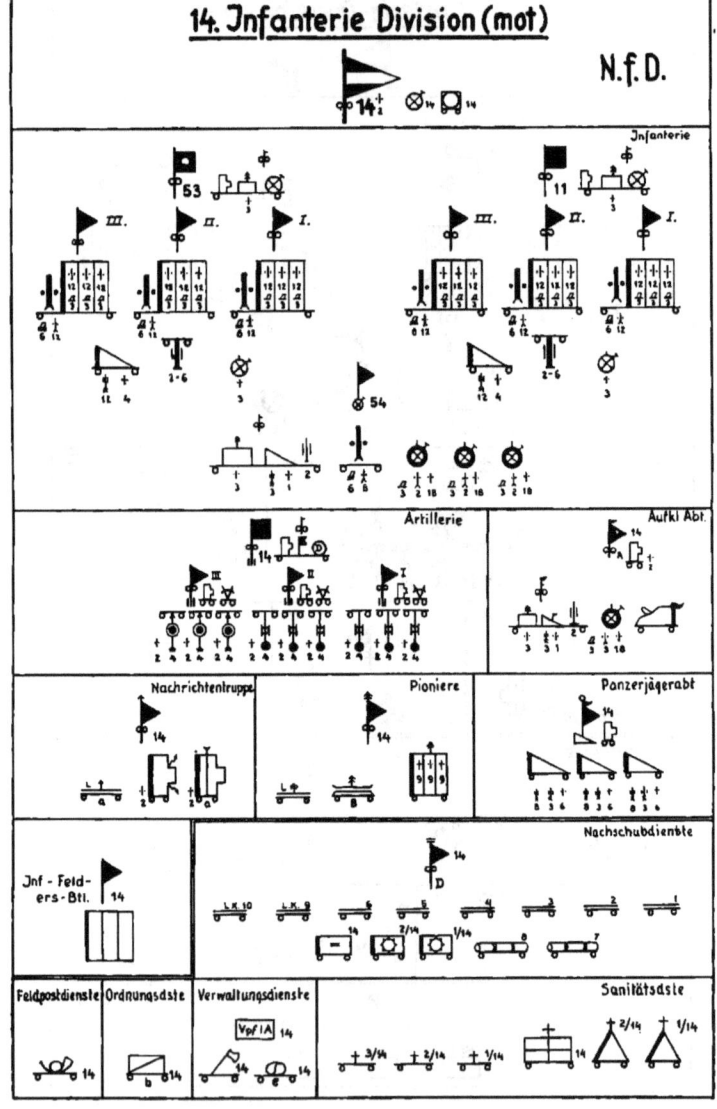

DOCUMENTS

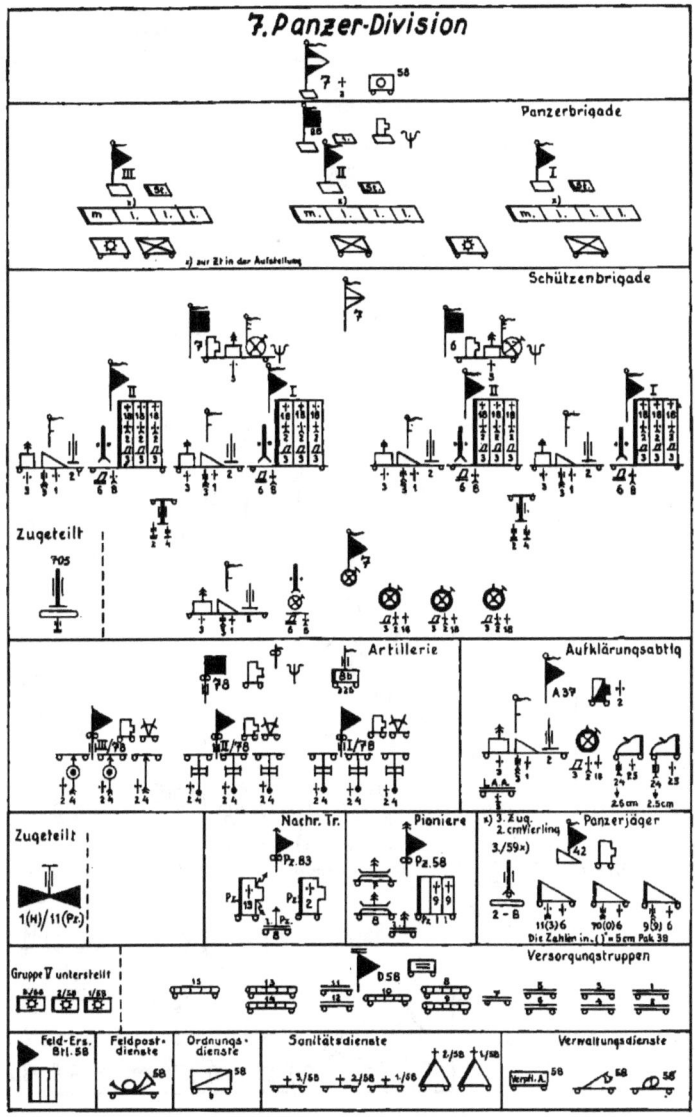

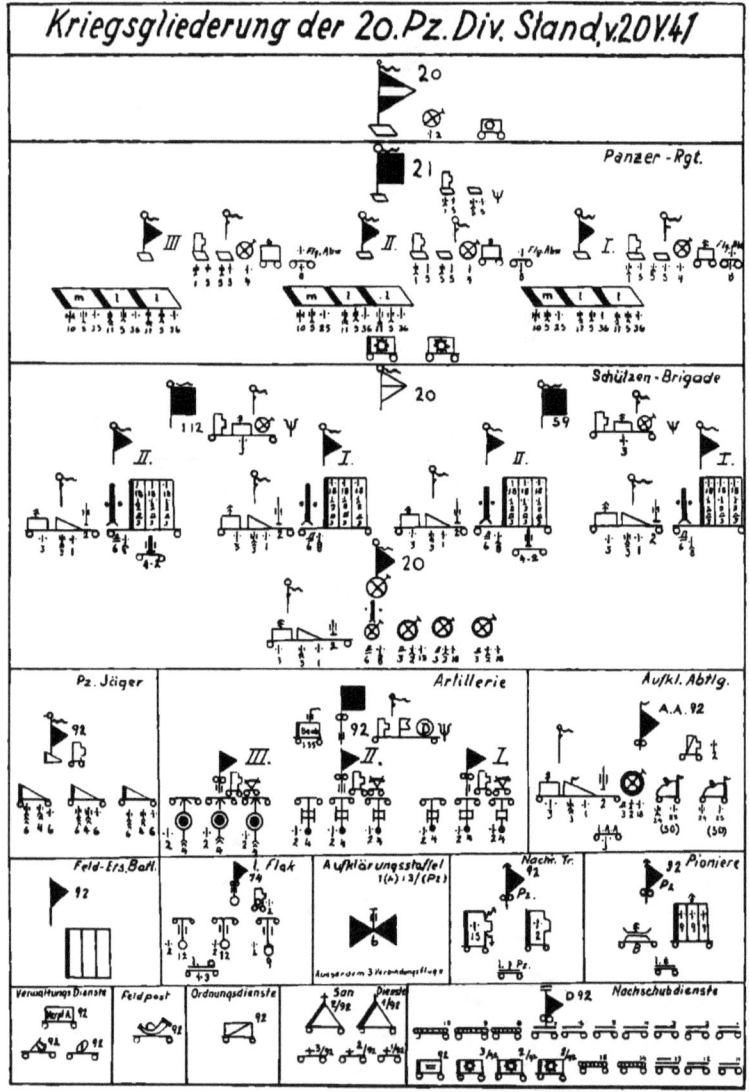

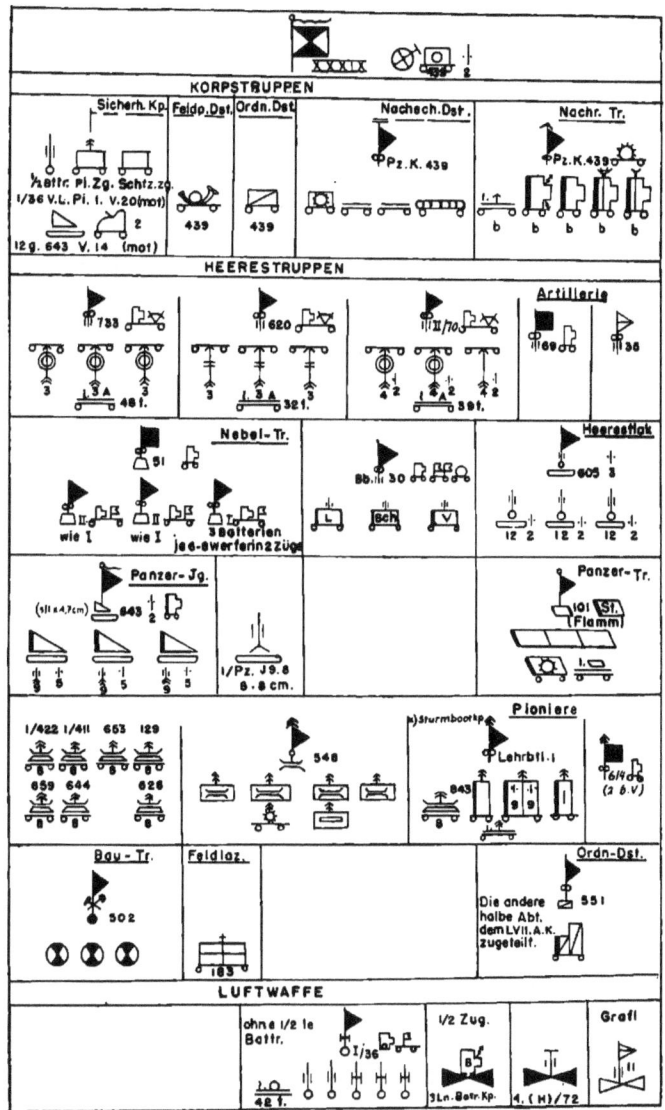

Gen St d H H Qu., den 7.5.1940
Op. Abt.(III)
Nr. 302/40g.Kdos.

Chef-Sache!
Nur durch Offizier!

Gliederung und Stellenbesetzung „Fall Gelb"

—— Stand am 1.5.1940 ——

Verteiler:

Adj. Ob d H	1.	Ausfertigung
Adj. Chef Gen St d H	2.	"
Adj. O Qu I	3.	"
Adj. O Qu II	4.	"
Op. Abt. Chef	5.	"
Ia	6.	"
I	7.	"
Ia	8.	"
IIb	9.	"
III	10.	"
	11.	"
6 Z	12. u. 13.	"
P.A. (Chef)	14.	"
P.A. (Oberst Westhofen)	15.	"
Adj. d. Führers	16.	20 Ausfertigungen
Vorrat	17.	2.Ausfertigung
	18.	"
	19.	"
	20.	"

Geheime Kommandosache

Wer in einer geheimen Gegenstand im Sinne des § 88 Reichs-Straf-Gesetzbuch (Fassung vom 24. April 1934). Zuwiderung wird nach den Bestimmungen dieser Gesetzes bestraft, sofern nicht andere Strafbestimmungen in Frage kommen.

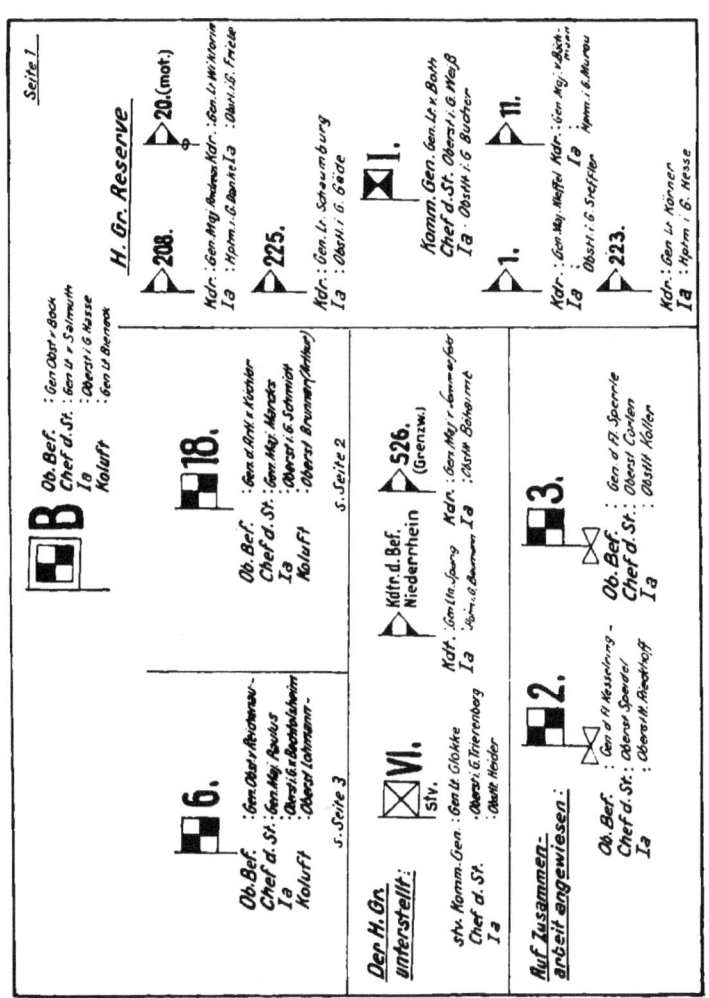

Seite 2

18. Komm. Gen: Gen.d.Art.v.Küchler
Chef d.St.: Gen.Maj. Marcks
I a : Oberst i.G. Schmidt
Koluft : Oberst Brunner (Arthur)

X. Komm. Gen: Gen.Lt. Hansen (Christ.)
Chef d.St.: Oberst i.G. Gause
I a : Oberstlt. i.G. Linnebein

227. Kdr: Gen. Maj. Zickwolff
I a : Hptm. i.G. Graf v. Bismarck-Schönhausen

SS "A.H." Kdr: SS Ob.Gr.f. Dietrich

207. Kdr: Gen.Lt. v. Tiedemann
I a : Oberstlt. v. Zitzewitz

SS "D.F." Kdr: SS Brrwf. F. Keppler

XXVI. Komm.Gen: Gen.d.Art. Wodrig
Chef d.St.: Oberstlt. i.G. Foertsch
I a : Maj. i.G. Montpour

9. Kdr: Gen. Maj. Hubicki
I a : Hptm. i.G. v. Mecoer

254. Kdr: Gen.Lt. Kast
I a : Major i.G. Zeicher

256. Kdr: Gen. Maj. Kauffmann
I a : Hptm. i.G. Deyhle (Aw)

Armeereserve:

SS "V" Kdr: SS Grupp.-Führer Hauser
I a : SS Stubf. F. Ostendorff

Kav. Rgt. 21 Kdr: Oberstlt. Frh. v. Boeselager

1. Kdr: Gen. Maj. Feige
I a : Maj. i.G. Oriani

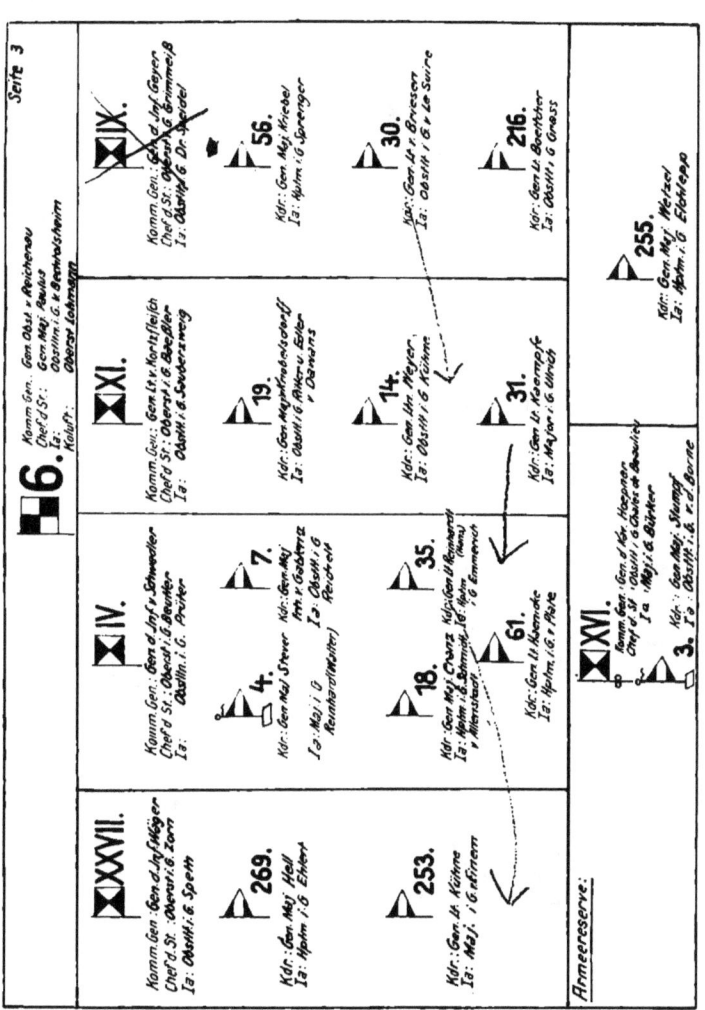

GERMAN MILITARY SYMBOLS

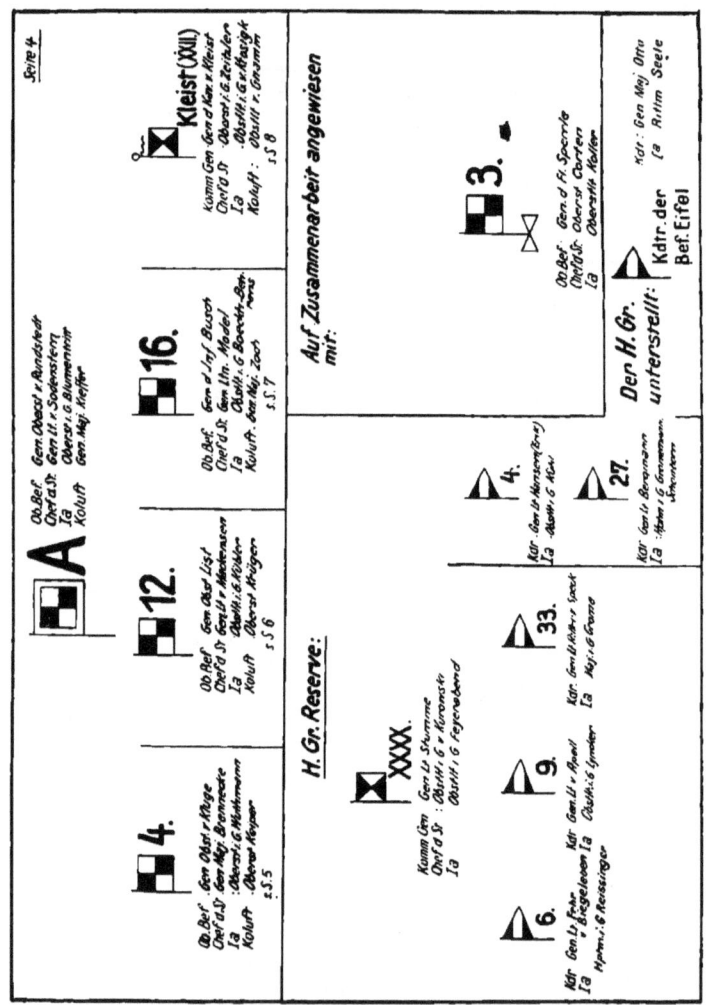

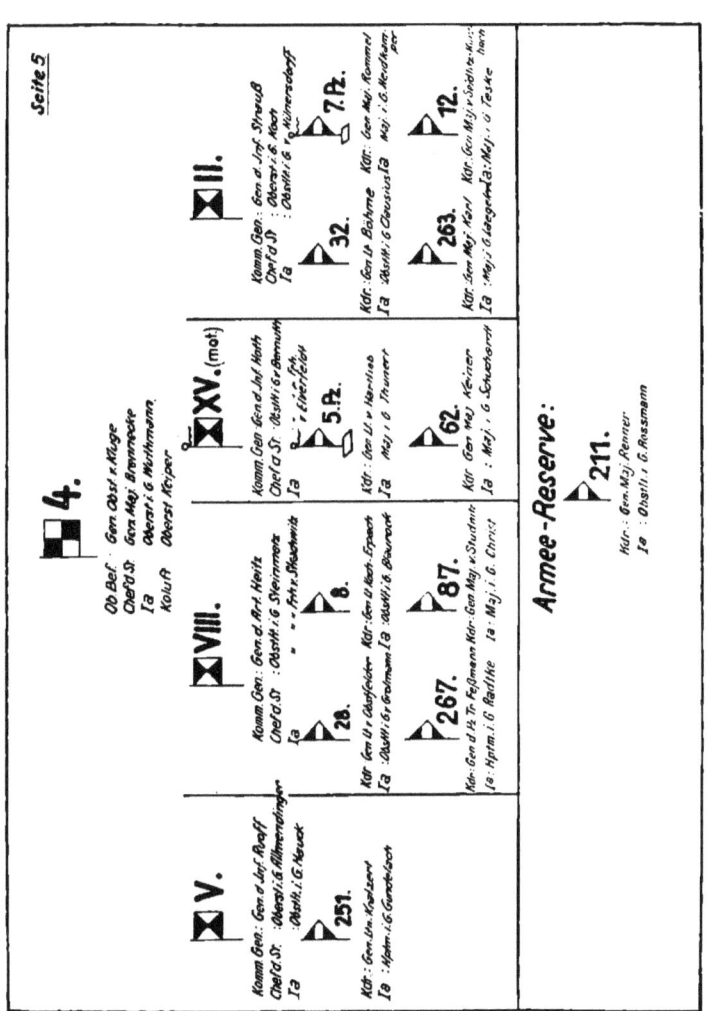

GERMAN MILITARY SYMBOLS

DOCUMENTS

291.
(Krys)
Kdr: Gen Maj Herzog
Ia: Hptm.i.G Müller (Christian)

297.
(Bruck/Leitha)
Kdr: Gen Lt Pfeffer
Ia: Hptm.i.G Brandt (Heinz)

292.
(Gr. Bonn)
Kdr: Gen Maj Urhmel
Ia: Maj.i.G Obermayer

noch O.K.H Reserven

293.
(Frankf.Od.Küstrin)
Kdr: Gen Maj Russwurm
Ia: Hptm.i.G Petersen

298.
(Neuhammer)
Kdr: Gen Maj Graessner
Ia: Hptm.i.G Blumröder

296.
(Grafenwöhr)
Kdr: Gen Maj Stemmermann
Ia: Hptm.i.G Leuthessen

Seite 15

299.
(Ohrdruf)
Kdr: Gen Maj Moser
Ia: Hptm.i.G Meyer-Detring

In Aufstellung:

XXXXIII.
(Hannover)
Komm Gen
Chef d.St. Oberstl.i.G Schulz
Ia: Maj.i.G Knuppel

XXXXIV.
(Dresden)
Komm Gen
Chef d.St. Oberstl.i.G Sixt
Ia: Maj.i.G Sittmann

XXVIII.
(W.K.III)
Komm Gen
Chef d.St.
Ia

XXIX.
(W.K.IV)
Komm Gen
Chef d.St.
Ia

XXXVI.
(W.K.X)
Komm Gen
Chef d.St.
Ia

XXXVII.
(W.K.XI)
Komm Gen
Chef d.St.
Ia

XXXVIII.
(W.K.XII)
Komm Gen
Chef d.St.
Ia

XXXIX.
(W.B.Prag)
Komm Gen
Chef d.St.
Ia

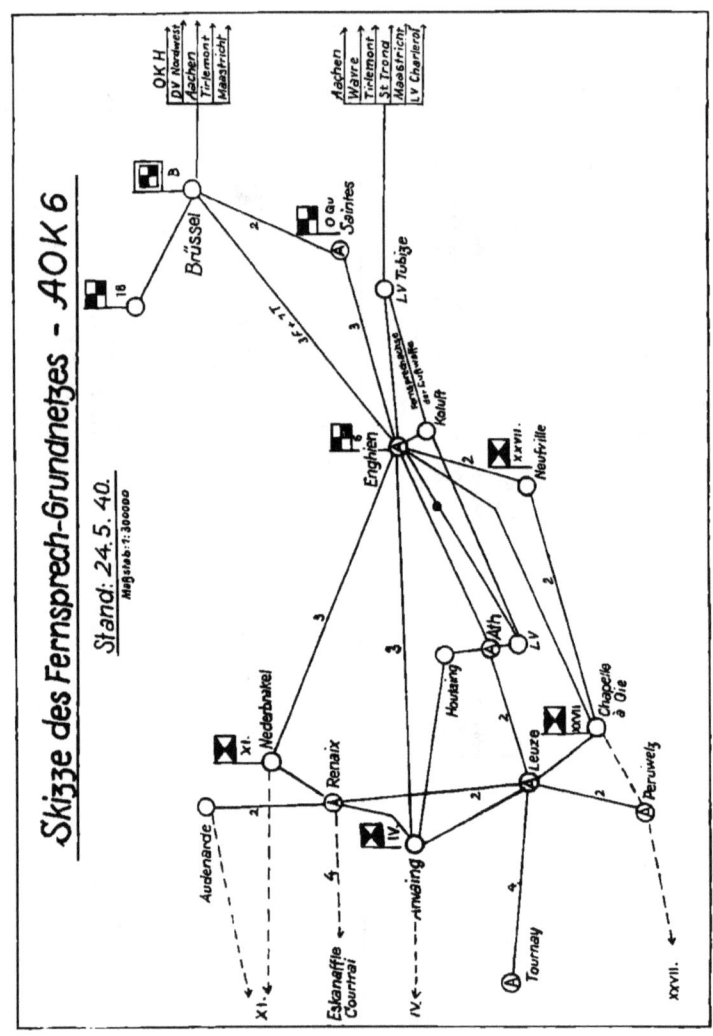

ADDENDA

The following military symbols arrived too late to be included in the section devoted to antiaircraft artillery.

Military Symbol	German	U. S. Equivalent
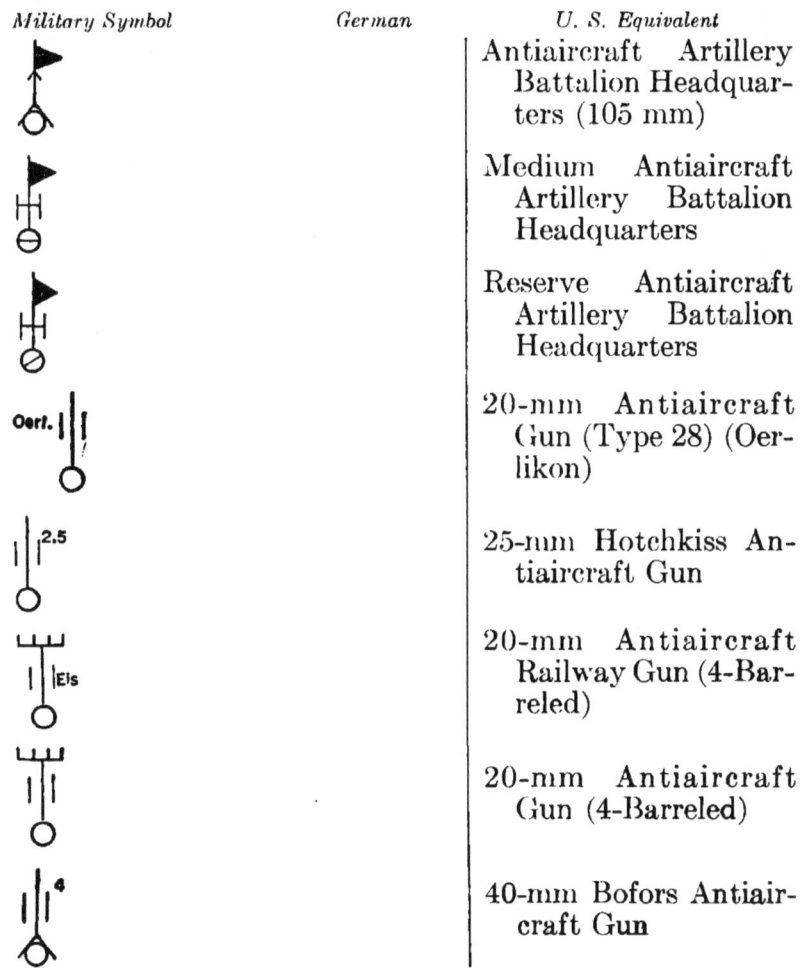		Antiaircraft Artillery Battalion Headquarters (105 mm)
		Medium Antiaircraft Artillery Battalion Headquarters
		Reserve Antiaircraft Artillery Battalion Headquarters
		20-mm Antiaircraft Gun (Type 28) (Oerlikon)
		25-mm Hotchkiss Antiaircraft Gun
		20-mm Antiaircraft Railway Gun (4-Barreled)
		20-mm Antiaircraft Gun (4-Barreled)
		40-mm Bofors Antiaircraft Gun

144 GERMAN MILITARY SYMBOLS

Captured 75-mm Antiaircraft Gun M 36 (French)

Barrage Gun (Caliber to be Shown on Right of Symbol)

Reserve 88 mm Antiaircraft Gun

Fixed Medium Antiaircraft Gun

www.ingramcontent.com/pod-product-compliance
Lightning Source LLC
Chambersburg PA
CBHW070157100426
42743CB00013B/2948